Virginia Indians at Werowocomoco

A National Park Handbook

Captain John Smith Chesapeake National Historic Trail

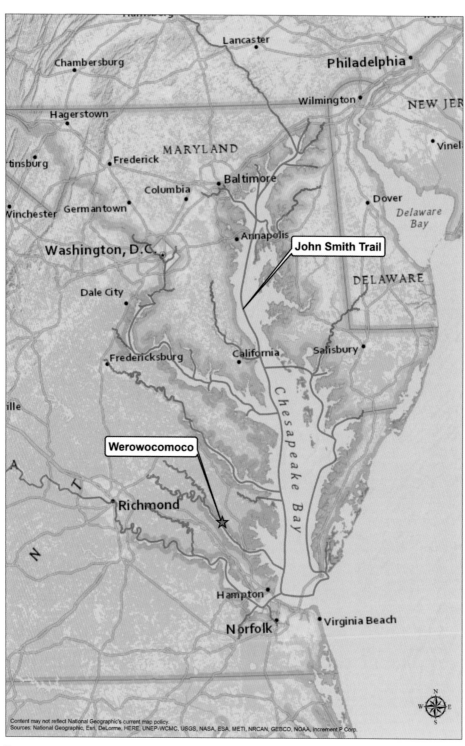

Virginia Indians at Werowocomoco

A National Park Handbook

Lara Lutz
Martin D. Gallivan
E. Randolph Turner III
David A. Brown
Thane Harpole
Danielle Moretti-Langholtz

The Captain John Smith Chesapeake National Historic Trail travels nearly 3,000 miles across the Chesapeake Bay and its rivers. The trail was officially launched in 2007 as part of the 400th anniversary of the founding of Jamestown, Virginia. Since then, the trail has been extended beyond the route of Smith's explorations to include the rivers and upper reaches of rivers that served as trade and transportation routes for Indian tribes who lived here before the English arrived.

About this Book:

At the time of this publication, the archeological site of Werowocomoco, located in Gloucester County, Virginia, is privately owned and under a preservation easement held by the Virginia Board of Historic Resources of the Virginia Department of Historic Resources. This book, part of the National Park Service Handbook series, is the result of a partnership between the National Park Service and the Virginia Department of Historic Resources, in collaboration with the Werowocomoco Research Group and the Virginia Indian Advisory Board for Werowocomoco.

The partners thank the following organizations and individuals for their assistance with this publication: The Colonial Dames of America/Chapter XXIII-Virginia; Fairfield Foundation; Virginia Museum of Natural History Foundation; Jamestown-Yorktown Foundation; Pamunkey Museum; Bob Ripley for his wonderful photographs including those that open each chapter; Jessica Stewart for her early work organizing images for the book; Elizabeth Leclerc at ArcPoint Indexing; and at the Virginia Department of Historic Resources, the following individuals: Mike Barber, Dominic Bascone, Dee DeRoche, Karen Hostettler, Patty Hurt, Elizabeth Reighard, Stephanie Williams, and a special thanks to now-retired DHR archeologist Randy Turner.

For more acknowledgments, please see page 126.

Printed in the United States of America by McDonald & Eudy Printers, Inc.

ISBN: 978-0-692-42219-9

Cataloging-in-Publication information available upon request to the Virginia Department of Historic Resources

Cover Illustrations: The cover presents an artist's bird's-eye view of Werowocomoco around the late 1500s, prior to the arrival of Europeans in present-day Virginia in 1607. The illustration is both conjectural (e.g., the placement of huts along the river, the location where canoes were beached, or the extent of the woods and tree line) and based on recent archeological research (e.g., the location of a chief's longhouse toward the rear of the site, the division of the site into "secular" and "sacred" areas) and contemporary scholarship about Algonquian settlements.

The inside cover illustration is also conjectural, although it also reflects contemporary scholarship about the construction of native dwellings and the activities of the Algonquian people and their lifeways in a settlement just prior to the arrival of Europeans. (NPS-VDHR illustrations)

Contents

Forewords:

National Park Service
Virginia Department of Historic Resources
Werowocomoco Research Group
Pamunkey Indian Tribe

National Park Service

Werowocomoco is an extraordinary place. Although there were multiple early interactions between the English and the American Indians, the first recorded meetings between an American Indian leader and leaders of the first permanent English colony took place here. Until the recent discovery of the site of Werowocomoco, our knowledge has been limited to brief references in the writings of the English newcomers. Now the other side of the story is being revealed, as archeology gradually chips away the layers of mystery surrounding the indigenous people of this land. For American Indians, particularly the Virginia Indians descended from the Algonquian-speaking native nations of this area, the discoveries provide tangible evidence of their heritage. For visitors, it is a place of discovery that can lead to greater understanding of the origins of what became the United States of America.

At Werowocomoco, many thoughtful people have come together to work on how best to preserve, study, and share their stories of what happened here. The National Park Service is honored to partner with the Virginia Department of Historic Resources, the landowners, the Werowocomoco Research Group, and its Virginia Indian Advisory Board on this publication.

But the story of Werowocomoco is not easy to tell, in part because so very little is known about what sort of world the English entered. Today there are only two types of scholarly primary source information about Werowocomoco. One is the accounts written by English colonists, of which only Captain John Smith was known to have been at the site. His writings of visiting Werowocomoco were authored at different times, and are not always consistent with each other. Furthermore the perspective of the English was colored by their own worldview, so that they saw the native world and its societies through their own old-world lens.

The other scholarly primary source is a fascinating and slowly growing body of archeological research, which holds great promise for additional information in the future. Both the historical records left by the English and the archeological research being done today require interpretations by scholars and others, and not all of those who have studied the same source materials will agree on those interpretations.

Although the Virginia Indian tribes who had a relationship with Powhatan had no written languages and therefore could not leave a written record, the views of their descendants more than 400 years later are essential. In addition there are the views of other American Indians and native people, who understand how the events connected to Werowocomoco were exemplary of European attempts to colonize indigenous peoples and their lands.

We can see that a brief publication could never show the complexity of the American Indians and English interactions that took place at Werowocomoco. In this handbook we have chosen to tell the basics of the primary source material about this special place, including some scholarly interpretation for a general audience, and provide the opportunity for the reader to explore further. We have generally tried to avoid anthropological terms and have provided a glossary and references for additional reading. We hope the reader will wish to learn more from the various partners and from the site itself, because Werowocomoco— scarcely explored archeologically—still holds its secrets and promises, and its story belongs to the ages. We are immensely thankful to the Virginia tribes for greatly enhancing this work through their active participation and contributions.

Chuck Hunt
Superintendent
National Park Service–Chesapeake

Virginia Department of Historic Resources

Asked to name landscapes in the U.S. today associated with American Indians before European settlement in North America, many people would cite Canyon de Chelly in the Southwest or Medicine Wheel-Medicine Mountain in Wyoming—or another place encompassing a sweeping prairie scene, mountain vista, or canyon in the American West.

People rarely think about American Indian landscapes in the eastern half of the country; fewer still of a specific Virginia landscape—unless they know the story of Werowocomoco, a roughly 50 acre archeological site in Gloucester County, Virginia.

It's a special—and for many Virginia Indians today, a spiritual—place, situated along Virginia's scenic York River, now part of the Captain John Smith Chesapeake National Historic Trail. A visitor there can vividly imagine how it may have appeared 800 or more years ago when archeologists tell us Werowocomoco was already an important American Indian settlement. Yes, changes to the shoreline have occurred and a modest modern house and secondary building stand on a compact portion of the site, but essentially it remains as it was in the pre-Contact era: a broad open terrace gently inclining away from the tidal waters of the York River's Purtan Bay, a peninsula bounded by creeks, wetlands, and woods.

Werowocomoco, in this regard, is a rarity in Virginia: a relatively undisturbed American Indian cultural landscape. (For readers unfamiliar with the term, cultural landscape is "a geographic area, including both cultural and natural resources," according to the National Park Service, that is "associated with a historic event, activity, or person or exhibiting other cultural or aesthetic values.")

Drive Virginia's Scenic Highways or follow our many Heritage Trails and you'll see layers of cultural landscapes. The towns and farms of 19th-century Shenandoah Valley, the colonial era plantations of the James River, the coal mines and railroad towns of western Virginia, the bright leaf tobacco barns in the fields of Southside, or our preserved Civil War battlefields are just a few examples.

Last occupied by chief Powhatan in 1609, Werowocomoco's American Indian cultural elements have long vanished from above ground. Yet during the four centuries since 1609, the land was farmed, a low-impact activity that has left much of Werowocomoco's archeological features largely undisturbed below the plow zone so far as we know. (The property's owners voluntarily prohibited plowing beginning in 2003.)

Today Werowocomoco offers a deeply embracing and evocative intimacy and promises to reveal through continued archeological research much more about the settlements and lifeways of the Algonquian people who occupied the site for at least 400 years prior to the arrival of the English at Jamestown.

For this book, we worked with the archeologists and representatives of the Virginia Indian tribes closely affiliated with Werowocomoco and the scholarship of Virginia's Algonquian people to create two illustrations that envision the site prior to European contact. While much is conjecture in the illustrations, much is based on current research, which this book details. For now, they provide an imaginative glimpse—subject to revision as research continues —of how this cultural landscape may have looked when it was a place of secular and sacred importance to Virginia's Algonquian people, who were called the Powhatan by English settlers.

So, welcome to Werowocomoco by way of this book—a place worthy of far greater recognition among the many, many storied and historic places of Virginia, where people have been living for upwards of 16,000 years.

Julie V. Langan
Director, Virginia Department of Historic Resources

Werowocomoco Research Group

On an icy afternoon in February 2003, fog hung over Purtan Bay, clinging to the sentinel pines on shore as the native delegations reached Werowocomoco. An archeological survey had uncovered evidence that the riverine terrace overlooking Purtan Bay held the remains of a sprawling native town. We invited tribal leaders and representatives of local tribes, descendants of the American Indians who constructed the town centuries earlier, to see the location firsthand and to discuss potential collaborative work there. Though visibility was limited that winter day, looking back it is clear that the moment was right for collaborative study of native landscapes in the Chesapeake.

The survey, conducted by Fairfield Foundation archeologists David Brown and Thane Harpole in consultation with Virginia Department of Historic Resources archeologist Randy Turner, recovered evidence that the site was indeed Werowocomoco, the Powhatan political center. Scholars had long sought to pin down the site's whereabouts. As early as the 19th century historians compared colonial maps with accounts of the town's location to determine that Werowocomoco was most likely situated along Purtan, a broad bay on the York River. Recognizing that excavations at the site would likely produce results significant to several different communities, Randy, Dave, and Thane invited William and Mary faculty members Martin Gallivan and Danielle Moretti-Langholtz to join them on a team we dubbed the Werowocomoco Research Group.

The site's location and artifacts match details from Werowocomoco's earliest written accounts. Lynn Ripley, who owns the property with her husband Bob, had for years collected materials from plow-disturbed areas and from the eroding bluff along the riverfront. These included native ceramics, stone tools, glass beads, and copper sheeting associated with a late prehistoric through early colonial settlement. While much scholarship and heritage work in Tidewater Virginia has focused on the English colonial world, Lynn's collection brought to light a native landscape with a much deeper history.

Representatives from the six Virginia tribes who visited the site on that icy afternoon in 2003 agreed to partner with us in a study of the site. The tribes formed an advisory board to the project with representatives who have since met to discuss research designs, funding options, and reporting protocols. William and Mary archeology students have also played a central role in this effort, investing thousands of hours in the field and laboratory. The resulting collaboration brought together students, scholars, Virginia tribes, and the property owners for a long-term study of the site.

This volume summarizes the results of these partnerships, offering a broadly accessible narrative of Werowocomoco, past and present. We have many to thank for helping us bring this story to the public. Lara Lutz has done an extraordinary job translating the technical details of the research for this book. The Ripleys have been our generous and patient hosts for well over a decade. Funding has come from many sources, including the National Endowment for the Humanities, the Virginia Foundation for the Humanities, the National Park Service, the College of William and Mary, and the Virginia Department of Historic Resources. Above all, our partners in the native community have made this project possible, in part by guiding us toward key research questions aimed at native histories beyond the colonial encounter.

Werowocomoco Research Group

David A. Brown
Martin D. Gallivan
Thane Harpole
Danielle Moretti-Langholtz
E. Randolph Turner III

Pamunkey Indian Tribe

Some tribes referred to pages in a book as "talking leaves."

The leaves that fell and covered the ground at Werowocomoco have remained silent and undisturbed, waiting to talk for centuries.

Now it is time to listen.

Listen to the drum beat; listen to the children's feet, the sentinel's call, a chief's oratory, or the crack of a stone shattered to make a tool.

All this and more was heard and done 400 years before John Smith landed at Jamestown, and now 400 years later the leaves are finally telling their story.

It's a story of power, of politics, war, suffering, and conquest. It's also a story of a fragile paradise lost, lost within one generation.

Now, we the descendants of the Algonquian people that inhabited this paradise have a chance to sit and scrape, with trowels and shovels in the sacred earth of our Tsenacomoco. Waiting to uncover a flake of stone or piece of copper that might "talk to us."

What is it saying?

It's telling us to be proud, be curious, be respectful and imaginative. It's telling us to not forget the destruction of our culture, and the treachery we suffered at the hands of the English settlers. It's also telling us that friendship, cooperation and time can heal old wounds. Wounds that have remained for 400 years, just under the surface, like the artifacts at Werowocomoco.

Chief Kevin Brown, Pamunkey

Werowocomoco

[WAYR-uh-wah-KOH-muh-koh]

Chapter 1
Werowocomoco: A Place of Power

On February 15, 2003, a parcel of land along Virginia's York River was wrapped with the quiet of a deep winter day, save for a breeze off the river that picked up speed as the sun traveled the sky. Across the fields, along the woods and the shoreline of Purtan Bay, the human footsteps of a small gathering made history. Virginia Indians, representing seven tribes, were among this group, marking the largest—and possibly first—native presence at this site in some 400 years. Yet Indians had hunted, fished, and raised families on this land for thousands of years. Over time, it became a seat of power for Virginia Indians and the site of interactions with European colonists that would reshape lives for generations to come. This place was and, in many ways, remains Werowocomoco.

More than 400 years before English settlers established Jamestown, Werowocomoco had been an important Powhatan Indian settlement. Werowocomoco, translated from the Virginian Algonquian language, means "place of leadership." As an archeological site, Werowocomoco was confirmed in 2002, nearly 400 years after the Indian leader paramount chief Powhatan and his people interacted with Jamestown settlers here and at Jamestown. The site is located along the York River's Purtan Bay, in Gloucester County, Virginia. (Photo: John Henley)

On today's maps, Werowocomoco can be found in Gloucester County, Virginia, on the north side of the York River. Nothing above ground remains of the Indian community that existed here. The rural landscape is largely intact, however, and clues to the past still lie in the earth. Fields and forests at the site surround a private, single-family home, situated at the end of a long gravel road with a view of Purtan Bay and the York River beyond. In the early 1600s, this river was known as the Pamaunke, and today some believe that Werowocomoco was a political and spiritual center in the Tidewater Indian world.

Indians moved away from Werowocomoco in 1609, and the land has been in private hands since colonial times. In the centuries that followed, Indian heritage was both neglected and suppressed. While historians and others kept the memory of Werowocomoco alive, knowledge of its story faded. Scholars of indigenous cultures still associated the settlement with the north shore of the York River, but its exact location was no longer clear.

And then, in 2001, Werowocomoco surfaced once again. Archeologists Thane Harpole and David Brown of the Fairfield Foundation paid a visit to Bob and Lynn Ripley, who lived on the York River at Purtan Bay. Lynn Ripley had an impressive collection of artifacts from her land. The Ripleys' garage was a workspace for sorting pottery fragments and projectile points, most of which she had gathered from the eroding shoreline. Harpole and Brown, who knew that Werowocomoco might have been at this location, immediately saw the significance of the artifacts. They contacted Randolph Turner, an archeologist at the Virginia Department of Historic Resources. Their exchange was the start of a partnership between the Ripleys, archeologists, and Virginia's Indian communities. Together, this partnership has restored native connections to Werowocomoco and directed respectful scholarship to the deep history of the site.

A detail from a famous 1612 John Smith map of "Virginia,"
as the English called the region, shows how closely situated
were Jamestown and Werowocomoco—as the crow flies,
only about 15 miles distant. The powerful political and spiritual
leader known as Wahunsenacawh (Powhatan) was residing
at Werowocomoco when Smith was brought before him as a
prisoner. It was at Werowocomoco that Smith also crossed paths
with Wahunsenacawh's young daughter, Matoaka (Pocahontas),
according to Smith's later accounts.

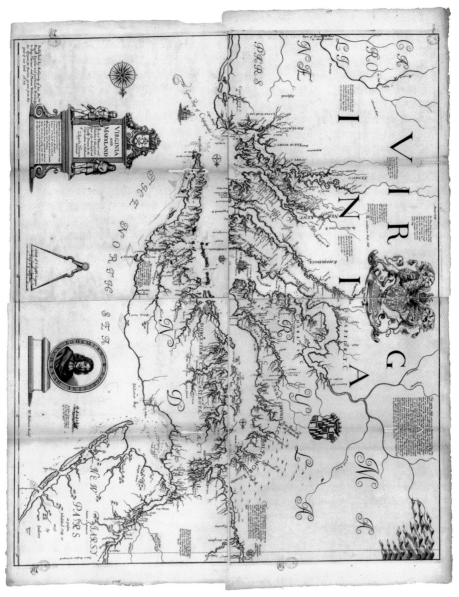

A map from 1670 by Augustine Herman shows the Chesapeake Bay region. Place names are noted with English and American Indian words. Werowocomoco, however, is not one of the place names. By the time this map was made, Werowocomoco had mostly vanished from written records of the day. (Library of Congress)

Werowocomoco—translated in the general sense from the Virginia Algonquian language as "place of leadership"—was the residence of a powerful political and spiritual leader known as Powhatan. His daughter Pocahontas could be found there too. Scholars believe that, beginning in the late 1500s, Powhatan established a chiefdom that may have influenced dozens of communities and their leaders along the rivers of the southern Chesapeake Bay. Among them were the ancestors of several contemporary Virginia tribes, including the Pamunkey, Mattaponi, Upper Mattaponi, and likely the Nansemond and Rappahannock as well. The Chickahominy were located near the center of the chiefdom but remained independent of it and did not pay tribute to Powhatan.

Looking across the site of Werowocomoco today. The York River is just visible beyond the trees. (Photo: Bob Ripley)

In the spring of 1607, English colonists arrived on a neighboring river, now named the James. A few Europeans had explored the Chesapeake before, but this was a larger group and they aimed to stay. The colonists built a stockade on the edge of a swamp and named it James Fort. It would soon become Jamestown, the first permanent English settlement in North America. But in the early 1600s, the future of the colonists, the Virginia Indians, and what would become the United States was not only unwritten but very much uncertain. Within a span of decades, their stories would change dramatically. The people who walked the shores of Werowocomoco witnessed events that Indians, scholars, and curious visitors continue to ponder and question today.

Captain John Smith, an English leader of James Fort, wrote that he met Powhatan and Pocahontas when he was captured and brought to Werowocomoco in December 1607. Their meeting marked the beginning of escalating interactions between Indians and colonists that ranged from cautious and friendly to confusing and violent. By 1609, more of the English had arrived and continued to demand food from the Indian harvests. The Indians were increasingly unwilling to trade and wary of English intentions. Attempts at cooperation steadily led to conflict, and Powhatan moved his headquarters farther inland. Werowocomoco soon fell silent.

The land at Werowocomoco was then cultivated for crops and timber from the early days of colonial Virginia, either by a single family or small cluster of neighbors. There is no indication that they maintained any direct association of the land with Werowocomoco or its importance to native and colonial history. Through the centuries, its identity as a native place echoed mostly through the ink of colonial explorers, who had recorded its location on hand-drawn maps and in personal accounts of events in and near the site. The Indian perspective on Werowocomoco was not documented, and its story was largely overshadowed by the unfolding of a new nation that, in celebrating its own history, often dismissed the history of those who preceded it.

Now, through a remarkable confluence of people, funding, research, and partnerships, Werowocomoco has begun to receive the attention it deserves. Its location has been pinpointed, explored, and honored. The Ripleys not only permitted archeological explorations, but also welcomed them. Between 2003 and 2010, archeologist Martin Gallivan of the College of William and Mary led a series of field sessions supported not only by

A ceremony was held at Werowocomoco on June 21, 2013, to officially recognize the preservation easement for the site that the property's owners, the Ripleys, had donated to the Commonwealth of Virginia. During the ceremony the chiefs of Virginia's Powhatan-descendant tribes spoke. Pictured L-R, from top to bottom, are Chief Stephen R. Adkins, Chickahominy Indian Tribe; Chief Gene "Pathfollower" Adkins, Chickahominy Indians Eastern Division; Chief Mark "Falling Star" Custalow, Mattaponi Indian Reservation; Chief G. Anne Richardson, Rappahannock Tribe; Chief Kenneth Adams, Upper Mattaponi Indian Tribe, and Chief Kevin Brown, Pamunkey Indian Tribe, shaking hands with Douglas Domenech, Virginia's Secretary of Natural Resources at the time, with owners Bob and Lynn Ripley standing behind Brown. (Photos: Martin Sekula/VDHR)

William and Mary, but also by the Virginia Department of Historic Resources, National Park Service, and National Endowment for the Humanities. The fieldwork has revealed the deep history of Werowocomoco—a history now known to have begun centuries before Powhatan ever lived there.

The Werowocomoco research team established an important partnership with Virginia Indians, an effort led by William and Mary professor Danielle Moretti-Langholtz. As a result, the work at Werowocomoco is the first archeological project to take place with the sustained guidance and participation of Virginia Indians. The project's Virginia Indian Advisory Board includes representatives from the Pamunkey, Mattaponi, Upper Mattaponi, Rappahannock, Nansemond, and Chickahominy tribes. Together, they have provided advice and feedback on research goals, public outreach, and the handling of artifacts. Virginia Indians also helped with the field investigations, while others have come to walk the land, tour the excavations, and spend family time along the shore.

Long-term stewardship plans are in place for the site. In 2005 and 2006, Werowocomoco was added to the Virginia Landmarks Register and the National Register of Historic Places. In 2012, the Ripleys placed an easement on approximately 58 acres of the property through the Virginia Department of Historic Resources. The easement is a legal agreement, attached to the property deed, which helps provide permanent protection for the land and its archeological resources.

Protecting Werowocomoco, Now and in the Future

Approximately 58 acres of the Werowocomoco site received permanent protection in 2012, when the owners decided to place the land under a conservation easement administered by the Virginia Department of Historic Resources.

Conservation easements are legal agreements, created in partnership with a government agency or private organization, which set limits and conditions for the use and development of the land and which transfer with deed when a property is sold. Easement donations are entirely voluntary, and the terms of each easement are different, written to meet the needs of the landowners and the resources they aim to protect. Easements also offer financial benefits. Owners may be paid for their easements or receive tax benefits; others donate easements to the agency or organization that holds them.

The Virginia Department of Historic Resources has a long track record of creating successful conservation easements, and this experience helped secure permanent protection for Werowocomoco.

"Short of public ownership, a conservation easement is the best tool we have," said Kathleen S. Kilpatrick, who directed the Virginia Department of Historic Resources between 2001 and 2013. "It allows the property to be appropriately preserved while remaining on the tax rolls in the hands of private land owners."

Kilpatrick also steadfastly led the development of the Werowocomoco easement in addition to supporting archeological research at Werowocomoco through agency funding and dedicated staff time beginning in 2003. "Some aspects were unusual, but the effort was backed by a body of knowledge that the department has gained through many decades of experience, working through the nuts and bolts of easements," Kilpatrick said.

Virginia's easement program was established through state law in 1966. Since the first easement was negotiated in 1969, to date the department has administered nearly 600 easements on more than 38,000 acres of land. Easement properties range from less than 1 acre (many on city lots) to 1,000 acres, protecting historic estates, Civil War earthworks, gristmills, taverns, churches, factories, and more.

Archeological sites are protected by easements, too. Some, like Werowocomoco, safeguard the heritage and history of Virginia's first people. Cactus Hill in Sussex County contains evidence of human habitation dating back some 15,000 years. The Thunderbird Archeological District in Warren County protects sites dating to 9500 BCE, including the remains of what may be the oldest human structure in Virginia.

Bob and Lynn Ripley

Kathleen S. Kilpatrick at Werowocomoco. As director of the Virginia Department of Historic Resources, she led the agency in supporting archeological research at Werowocomoco and bringing the site under a historic preservation easement agreement with the Commonwealth of Virginia via the Department of Historic Resources. (Photos Bob Ripley)

11

Werowocomoco was an important addition to preserved properties in Virginia and the nation as a whole.

"I don't think you can walk the land without feeling the power of the place," Kilpatrick said. "Not only do people need to understand what took place there, they need to understand the complexity of the society it represented. It's a connection to our shared history and to the vibrancy of our Indian community today."

Creating an easement for Werowocomoco posed challenges because of the site's importance and the wide range of activities that could be desirable in the future. Most easements need to address the use of the property for homes and agriculture. Werowocomoco, however, is a large, dispersed archeological site of international importance. It might in time become a very open, active site, with a steady stream of visitors and facilities such as an archeology lab and welcome center.

The work toward an easement began by gaining a better understanding of the resources associated with the property. The Department of Historic Resources helped support the archeological explorations, which took place over several years. Bob and Lynn Ripley, the property owners, also invested time and resources in detailed property surveys to align its legal boundaries with the core area that would be protected by the easement.

Kilpatrick and the Ripleys shared many conversations about how the Ripleys hoped to use the property over the coming years and the protections that might be needed in the future should it pass to new owners.

"The Ripleys were wonderful to work with because they understand and honor stewardship as a value," Kilpatrick said. "They wanted to fit those values into their long-term goals for their family."

The final easement identifies five acres centered on the Ripleys' house where development changes can be made, such as renovations, enlargements, and demolitions that are compatible with the site.

"You have to find that sweet spot, the combination of good preservation and flexibility for the owner," Kilpatrick said. "I think we found it."

Looking to the future, Kilpatrick urged the Ripleys to consider the potential for additional archeological investigations, since only a small fraction of the total site has been studied to date. The type and volume of public access was a question too.

"What are the conditions and thresholds under which these types of activities could occur?" Kilpatrick asked.

The easement limits development to no more than one percent of the total area of the property. Along with defining a small area for residential development, the easement calls for the Virginia Department of Historic Resources to review and approve nearly all activities proposed for the property.

"It pretty much encompasses anything you might need for an open public historic site, but it's all subject to prior review and approval," Kilpatrick said.

The fate of artifacts uncovered at Werowocomoco, to date or in the future, was an important issue. The Ripleys maintain ownership of the artifacts while the land is in their hands, but they want the collection to stay intact. To achieve this, they agreed eventually to donate the collection to the Department of Historic Resources or to a museum or other organization approved by the department.

"These are not just artifacts," Kilpatrick said. "They are part of a culture and should be maintained together. The whole is greater than the sum of its parts."

Planning, negotiating, and finalizing the conservation easement for Werowocomoco was a five-year process.

"Getting to the finish line depended on developing a good relationship with the Ripleys, finding commonality, and being patient," Kilpatrick said. "We recognized the supreme importance of this property and looked for the right time to move forward."

The announcement of the easement in 2012 was formally celebrated by the project partners, including the chiefs of today's Powhatan-descendant tribes, on June 21, 2013.

"An easement promises the property to the future," Kilpatrick said. "In that sense, this is an extremely optimistic and generous gesture. It's very powerful."

"The easement does what Lynn and I have done since the moment we learned that this land was Werowocomoco," said Bob Ripley. "It prohibits any penetration of top soil or subsoil without archeologists making excavations first."

Lynn Ripley said the easement has given them peace of mind that the property will be protected forever. "This is history we've been blessed to live on," she said. "We feel a strong responsibility to make sure it is here for generations to come."

Chapter 2
Life at the Water's Edge

When fall came to Werowocomoco, the sky over the river would darken with immense flocks of geese and ducks migrating south. In good years, fish like shad, sturgeon, and herring ran incredibly thick in nearby waters, signaling the arrival of spring and a relief from winter scarcity. Crabs thrived in the marsh grass, and oysters—enormous by today's standards—grew in crusty reefs, ready to harvest. Along the shore stood forest groves and a wide range of nuts, plants, and game. Deep, fertile soil provided rich ground for farming. While the water's edge has always rippled with life, American Indians who lived along these shores witnessed cycles of natural abundance that can only be imagined today.

American Indians preserved fish using smoke, which also flavored the meat. The image is from an engraving published in 1590 by Theodor de Bry. De Bry lived in what is now Belgium and made engravings of the watercolor paintings made by John White, an Englishman who was Governor of the ill-fated "Lost Colony" settled in 1584 in present-day North Carolina. The paintings of John White are significant because they offer the only eye-witness depictions of American Indian life at the time, although it is important to remember when viewing the images that Europeans had inherent misunderstandings or biases about American Indian culture that would shape their written and visual depictions of native culture. ("The Broiling of Their Fish Over the Flame," Theodor de Bry, from the collections of The Mariners' Museum, Newport News, Va.)

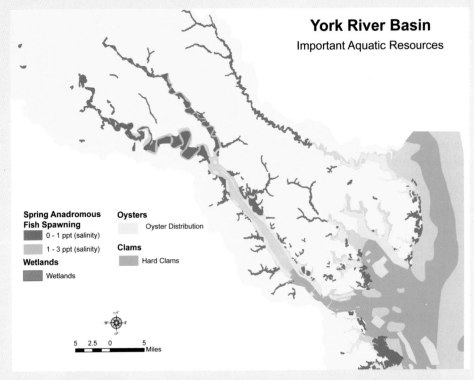

York River Basin
Important Aquatic Resources

Spring Anadromous Fish Spawning
- 0 - 1 ppt (salinity)
- 1 - 3 ppt (salinity)

Wetlands
- Wetlands

Oysters
- Oyster Distribution

Clams
- Hard Clams

5 2.5 0 5 Miles

(USGS/John Wolf)

The York River Basin's Aquatic Resources

Many fish species enter the lower York as part of their life cycle. Menhaden would have been visibly abundant in the seventeenth century, and due to the York's relative proximity (forty miles [64 kilometers]) to the mouth of the Chesapeake, striped bass, sea trout, drum, spot, croaker, and flounder. Up in the Pamunkey and Mattaponi rivers and their headwaters, resident freshwater species would have included bluegill, pickerel, and yellow and white perch, the latter moving down into the upper estuary, where their habitat overlapped that of striped bass.

The seasonal arrival of anadromous fishes [fish that migrate from saltwater to spawn in freshwater] would have been a signal event for American Indians during their hungriest season, the spring (winter stores used up, game animals with their fat used up, no berries available yet). They would have welcomed the shad and river herring fat with roe, bent on reproduction, streaming up the rivers and into the smallest freshwater creeks and rivulets. These species were abundant enough to be easy to harvest and were a rich source of calories as well as protein.

– from *John Smith's Chesapeake Voyages* 1607–1609
(University of Virginia Press, 2007)

The people of Werowocomoco, like those in each of the region's distinct political districts, lived with the rhythms of land and water. Their streams and rivers drained to the Chesapeake Bay, which takes its name from an Algonquian word first recorded in the 1580s to describe a place near the present-day cities of Virginia Beach and Norfolk.

The Chesapeake Bay is the United States' largest estuary, a place where fresh water from upland rivers mixes with salt water from the Atlantic Ocean. The rivers that drain into the Bay flow through an enormous area, or watershed, that includes much of Maryland and Virginia, parts of Pennsylvania, West Virginia, Delaware, and New York, and the entire District of Columbia. Water in the Bay, as well as the lower portions of its rivers, moves with the tide. In Virginia, the mostly low-lying land of these coastal areas, including the location of Werowocomoco, is known as the Tidewater.

Well over 15,000 years before the English colonists' arrival, small bands of people moved into the region to collect wild plants and hunt animals in an ice-age setting. As temperatures warmed and waters rose, the Chesapeake Bay began to take shape around the lower reaches of the ancient Susquehanna River. Archeology suggests that from about 900 CE to 1600 CE, Indian societies established larger, more permanent settlements along the Bay and began to grow corn, beans, and squash. The number and size of these communities apparently grew in the 1200s through 1500s.

Archeology tells a similar story at Werowocomoco. People were using the land at Purtan Bay at least 6,000 to 8,000 years ago. A town where people built homes, planted crops, and raised families began to develop in the 1200s—400 years before Europeans landed on nearby shores. Werowocomoco's archeology also indicates that the town stood apart from others. Evidence of Werowocomoco's unusual landscape (discussed in Chapter 8), combined with colonial-era accounts, suggest that the town represented an important ceremonial center with a long history and a place of power for the Virginia Algonquians.

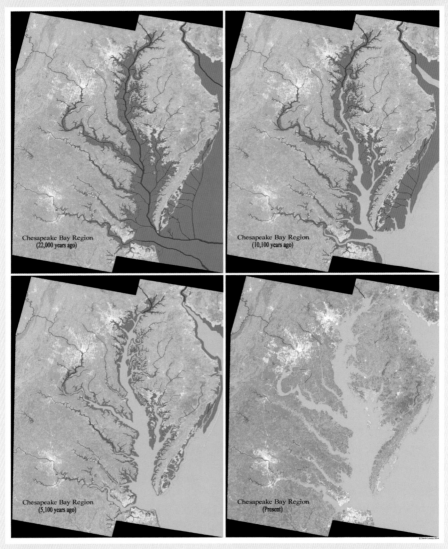

(Maps: Darrin Lowery)

During the past 22,000 years, at least 50 percent of the Delmarva Peninsula's uplands have been drowned by sea level rise. As a result, many of the earliest settlements, which were oriented near freshwater streams within higher-elevation forests, were slowly surrounded by shallow tidal waters. As the upland valleys were flooded, later peoples who settled on the surviving lands made use of the more-recently established environments provided by the shallow bays and tidal inlets. Eventually, even these later settlements were drowned by sea level rise; first, however, the settlements were covered by organic tidal marsh peat. Occurring over thousands of years, these natural processes and the rate of change with which they unfolded greatly influence how archeologists choose to investigate drowned archeological sites beneath the Chesapeake Bay and on the continental shelf of the Middle Atlantic region.

Atlantic sturgeon (Acipenser oxyrinchus). (USFWS/Duane Raver)

The Sturgeon

Imagine a fish rivaling the size of some of the sharks that course through the [Chesapeake] Bay. Then imagine this fish with a spadelike, upturned snout and bony plates that armor its sides and you have a link to the past; a fish whose heritage dates from some 200 million years ago. The Atlantic sturgeon was once quite common in the Chesapeake Bay and was the first "cash crop" at Jamestown. These primitive-looking fish can grow to ten feet (3 meters) or so and weigh several hundred pounds (over 300 kilograms)—yet these lumbering giants have been known to spring from the water and then flop back with a tumultuous splash.

Read the words of Nathaniel Hawthorne, who saw a sturgeon clear the water in Maine in 1837 and wrote: "I saw a great fish, some six feet long and thick in proportion, suddenly emerge at whole length, turn a somerset, its fins all spread, and looking very strange." Perhaps the Native Americans in Chesapeake Bay saw the same phenomenon. Another nineteenth-century writer recalled that "On the Potomac, during the Revolutionary war, one large sturgeon leaped into a ferry boat at Georgetown, coming down on the lap of an American officer with such violence as to break his thigh; the injury resulted in death."

– from *John Smith's Chesapeake Voyages* 1607–1609
(University of Virginia Press, 2007)

Werowocomoco was linked to the communities that paid tribute to Powhatan by a large network of rivers, streams, and smaller bays. In fact, it was usually easier to travel by water than by foot. Waterways supplied sustenance, too. Floodplain soil, nurtured by organic matter for thousands of years, helped the Indians raise crops of corn, beans, and squash. Fisheries were an excellent source of food. Alexander Whitaker, who came to Jamestown in 1611, reported: "The rivers abound with fish both small and great. The sea-fish come into our rivers in March … great schools of herring come in first; shads of a great bigness follow them." Nearly a hundred years later, historian Robert Beverley wrote, "In the spring of the year, herrings come up in such abundance … to spawn, that it is almost impossible to ride through, without treading on them."

Dugout Canoes

"Their canoes ... they make them with one tree ... in form of a trough. Some of them are an ell deep and 40 or 50 foot in length, but the most ordinary are smaller and will ferry 10 or 20 with some luggage over their broadest rivers. Instead of oars they use paddles and sticks with which they row faster than we in our barges."

– Captain John Smith, 1612

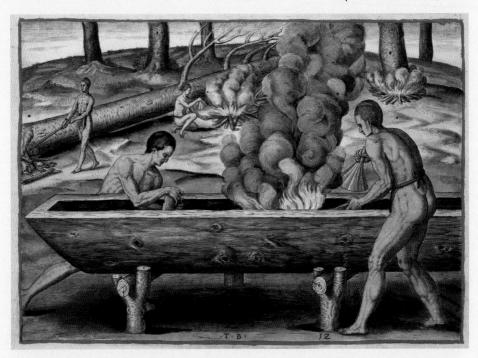

This de Bry engraving, also based on a John White watercolor, shows American Indians making a dugout canoe, using fire to hollow the log and then scraping away charred remains. (From the collections of The Mariners' Museum, Newport News, Va.)

American Indians in the Chesapeake Bay region relied heavily on dugout canoes for transportation. Dugout canoes were made from the trunks of large, straight trees. The largest were 40 or 50 feet long and 3 feet deep—big enough to carry 40 people. Strong, skilled paddlers were needed to steer them.

Making a dugout canoe took time and effort. The huge cypress and Atlantic white cedars that grew in the region would have been good choices for canoes because of their size and resistance to rot. Once a suitable tree was located, Indians would fell the tree by burning a fire at its base and chopping with stone axes. They then would float the tree to a work area.

To shape the tree into a canoe, Indians built small fires on the tree's surface and scraped away the charred wood with oyster shells. Mud, packed on the edges of the log, helped control the size and location of the fires. The cycle of burning and scraping would be repeated until the trunk was hollowed out and the bottom flattened to make the canoe stable in the water.

Park interpreters and visitors at Jamestown Settlement's re-created Powhatan Indian village use traditional American Indian methods of burning and scrapping away charred sections of a log to shape a canoe. (Photos: Jamestown-Yorktown Foundation)

Canoes of the Nansemond Indians, photographed by ethnographer Frank G. Speck, an early student of the "Father of American Anthropology" Franz Boaz. Speck conducted research trips for the Museum of the American Indian, Heye Foundation during the 1920s, visiting eastern Virginia's tribes including the Chickahominy, Mattaponi, Pamunkey, and Rappahannock in addition to the Nansemond. (Photo: Smithsonian National Museum of the American Indian)

The water's edge was a good place to be, but it was not without work or struggle. Disease and infections were facts of life. In the Chesapeake region, evidence suggests that few people lived beyond age 50, which was typical for the colonists, too. Rainfall varied from year to year and affected food supplies.

According to anthropologists, the people of this region understood their year as five seasons instead of four, reflecting the ways in which the landscape supported their diet and other community needs. In *cattapeuk* (early to mid-spring), they used weirs and nets to catch the migrating schools of shad, herring, and alewife. Turkeys and squirrels also provided protein, and the roots of a marsh plant called tuckahoe were a rich source of carbohydrates. Cattapeuk was also a time for planting crops and reaping young trees to build houses. For at least part of the season, the Indians would spread out from their towns to forage in outlying lands.

During *cohattayough* (mid-spring to mid-summer), people would be tending fields, hunting, foraging for plants and berries, and fishing—especially for large sturgeon. They began to harvest crops in *nepinough* (late summer to mid-fall) and gathered wild rice in the marshes. Corn harvesting continued during *taquitock* (late fall and early winter), along with feasts and religious

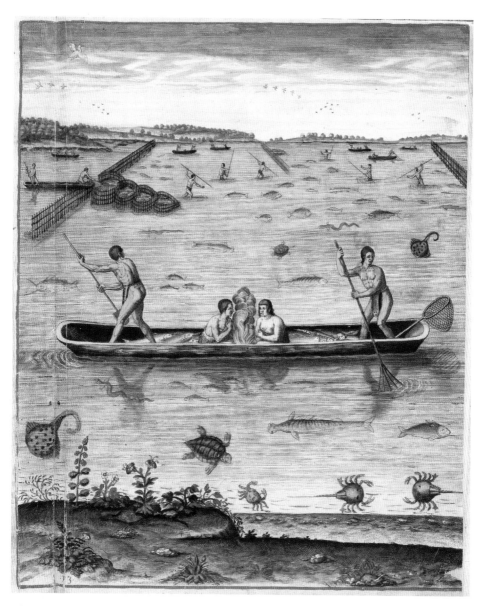

This de Bry engraving shows American Indians fishing with nets and weirs. A fire in the middle of the canoe attracts fish with its light. Weirs are shown in the background stretched across the water to trap fish. ("Their Manner of Catching Fish in Virginia," Theodor de Bry, from the collections of The Mariners' Museum, Newport News, Va.)

Tuckahoe or green arrow arum (Peltandra virginica) can be found in wetlands throughout the Eastern U.S. American Indians ate the leaves and roots of the plant, after thoroughly cooking it first. (Photo: Phillip Merritt)

rituals, until people dispersed to the forests to hunt deer and gather nuts. The greatest risk of hunger came during *popanow* (late winter and early spring), when options for game and foraging ran low. (For more on Algonquian words, see the Glossary on page 118.)

Indians knew a great deal about living within these cycles in order to provide enough food for their growing towns from one year to the next. But in the decades leading up to the founding of Jamestown, nature was making the job harder. A 1998 study of the Chesapeake region's climate history showed that the worst droughts of the past 800 years occurred during the late 1500s and early 1600s—just as English colonists at Roanoke and James Fort were struggling to survive. A Spanish Jesuit missionary who visited the area in 1570 described the land as "chastened" with famine and death.

Indians initially shared their crops with the needy newcomers at James Fort, but they did not have an endless supply. They were cautious and then resistant when the colonists' demands continued. The impacts of the drought—which stressed crops and brought fewer sturgeon to the river—made the situation dire for the English and pivotal for the Indians, who understood the value of their hard-earned food supply.

Chickahominy men fishing, photographed by Frank G. Speck. In the top photograph, Pamunkey leader George Major Cook (far right) is standing on the riverbank. Speck would stay with Cook, who served as Speck's guide, when the ethnographer visited the area. (Photos: Smithsonian National Museum of the American Indian)

Mattaponi men fishing on the Mattaponi Reservation, photographed by Speck, circa 1920s.

Pamunkey Chief George Major Cook, photographed by Speck, in 1920s. (Photos: Smithsonian National Museum of the American Indian)

Chapter 3
Indians of the Virginia Tidewater

Tsenacomoco, Chiskiack, and Orapax. Powhatan, Opechancanough, and Paspahegh. These are a few names, among countless thousands, that belonged to people and places in Tidewater Virginia before Europeans began to rewrite the map and alter the landscape. Colonists recorded some of the names they heard, trying their best to capture the sounds of Algonquian dialects with an English alphabet. We may never know exactly how these words should sound or the meanings, both direct and subtle, that would have been clear to a native speaker. But European attempts to record these words, especially on maps, begin to depict the extensive network of people and places that existed within the landscape.

When 104 men and boys arrived in 1607 to establish an English colony, they did not step onto an unnamed or unpeopled land. They arrived in an area that some Indians called *Tsenacomoco*, which is thought to mean "densely inhabited place." The Indian definition of Tsenacomoco is unclear, but anthropologists believe it roughly described the area of Tidewater Virginia or the area under Powhatan's influence.

At least 15,000 people lived in this region in at least 30 distinct groups that lined the southern shores of the Chesapeake Bay, its rivers, and some of their upper reaches. These groups varied in size, and each had a distinct identity. Most had at least one leader called a *werowance* or *werowansqua*. The Chickahominy, however, were led by a council whom the colonists described as "great men." During the late 1500s, many of these groups began paying tribute to Powhatan, who was a spiritual and influential leader. Powhatan was living at Werowocomoco when the English first met him in 1607.

Modern understanding of this world is intriguing, but incomplete. Indians did not have written records. There are no known writings that would help explain, in their words, their relationships with one another, their interactions with outsiders, their political organizations, or the rhythms and rituals of daily life.

American Indian Settlements of the Contact Period

Aspects of the Contact-period settlement that have already emerged through archeological investigations at Werowocomoco suggest a possible parallel use of space as illustrated in a John White watercolor of the North Carolina Algonquian settlement of Secota, reproduced here from a Theodor de Bry engraving.

The images from White and de Bry have been used to illustrate so many discussions of American Indian community organizations during the early colonial era that they have become iconic. Despite this overuse, the illustrations nonetheless are helpful for thinking about the organization of space within Contact-period Werowocomoco. White's paintings and de Bry's engravings have been characterized as Europeanized depictions of the native world in coastal North Carolina. No doubt this characterization has some truth, as may be seen in the fanciful wide, straight avenue running through Secota. Yet White's observations capture details that would otherwise be lost.

Like Secota, the Werowocomoco site includes a concentrated residential core located in close proximity to the riverfront. Moving away from the river (at top center) in the Secota image, an area of agricultural fields is followed by round plots for prayer, feasting, and ritual. Opposite the dance circle, a structure houses the remains of "kings and princes." Similarly, the interior zone of the Werowocomoco site includes trenches and other features that define an area of restricted access which were constructed several hundred years before the birth of Powhatan. Though these possible parallels between an Algonquian community in North Carolina and one in Virginia are suggestive, at this stage in the research they simply provide hypotheses for testing in future archeological investigations at the site. (From the collections of The Mariners' Museum, Newport News, Va.)

Secota by Theodor de Bry (From the collections of The Mariners' Museum, Newport News, Va.)

The knowledge that we now have about these communities derives from many other sources, and each has its limits. Like other peoples, Virginia Indians passed on memories and traditions through the generations but descendants are now centuries removed from the Powhatan era and no longer speak the Algonquian dialects of their ancestors. Early written accounts are laden with the racial and colonial bias of Europeans who experienced only fragments of the native world at a time when their culture and lifeways may have been, and certainly came to be, in crisis. Archeology uncovers direct evidence of past lives beyond the gaze of colonial chroniclers, but it reveals more about day-to-day activities than the ideas and understandings behind them. Still, each of these sources has important information to offer. Taken together, with thoughtful interpretation and conscious limits, possible threads of the story emerge, but they can be woven together in many ways.

Both archeology and colonial records show that the Indians of Tidewater Virginia lived in dispersed settlements. The settlements were not organized around main streets or market areas, but they united a defined community, with a central core near the water and dwellings and small cornfields spread out over the surrounding area. Their fluid boundaries make it difficult for researchers to locate and study the full extent of these settlements and to provide a complete picture of their size and distribution. The Indian cultural landscape also included places much farther from settled areas, where they would make seasonal visits to hunt game, harvest fish and oysters, and forage for useful plants. Each town usually had one or more leaders. Often one district had several towns, whereas others had just one.

Europeans called Indian homes "longhouses" because of their shape: they resembled elongated ovals with straight, parallel walls and rounded ends. The Indians called them *yihakans* or *ya'hacans*. The houses were built with sapling frames and covered with mats or bark. They typically ranged from 15- to 30-feet long and 10- to 18-feet wide. Some were more circular than oval. They had small openings for doorways and usually included a central hearth for cooking and providing heat. An opening in the roof allowed smoke to escape. Mats were hung to serve as walls or partitions,

especially in the large yihakans used by leaders. Archeology has found evidence that yihakans were built and rebuilt in the same locations over time, along with smaller, partially open shed-like structures where people could perform daily tasks in fresh air and good light.

Replicas of reed-covered longhouses at Jamestown Settlement. (Photo: Jamestown-Yorktown Foundation)

Powhatan may not have been the first strong leader to assert himself in Tsenacomoco, but he may have been the first to extend his reach so widely. Powhatan, whose personal name was Wahunsenacawh, was born about 1540 in a fortified town near the falls of the Powhatan (now James) River, near present-day Richmond. Historical documents indicate that Powhatan was of Pamunkey descent through his mother's side of the family.

According to information provided to Captain John Smith, Powhatan became a leader with an inheritance of six to nine districts. They included the Powhatan, Arrohateck, Appomattock, Pamunkey, Mattaponi, and Chiskiack.

This illustration offers a cutaway view in order to reveal how the interior of a typical longhouse may have appeared. As with the cover illustrations for this book, this one also is based on conjecture and scholarship. For instance, scholars are still unsure if these huts would have had a cover over the smoke hole at the top of the dwelling. Archeologists, however, have been able to determine the spacing between vertical supports based on postmolds uncovered at various archeological sites around Virginia, including Werowocomoco. (NPS-VDHR illustration)

Not Primitive at All: Indian Houses

The term "sapling-and-mat" houses makes many people think immediately of flimsiness and impermanence. The Algonquian speakers' houses were impermanent; they moved every few years anyway, and instead of selling or renting the "old" houses as modern mobile families do, they let theirs fall down—no one was going to occupy the sites for a while—and simply biodegrade.

The houses were not truly flimsy, though, as long as the pole framework's lashings were kept tight. Smaller houses were conical; longer houses had rounded ends that provided bracing. Such frameworks can withstand hurricane winds; although the mat or bark coverings would need repair or replacement afterward, the house would not be completely roofless. Such frameworks, especially the conical ones, can also withstand heavy snowfalls, which is why conical houses were standard among the northern Algonquian speakers from New England and the Canadian Maritime Provinces westward to the Great Lakes.

– Helen C. Rountree,
from *John Smith's Chesapeake Voyages 1607–1609*
(University of Virginia Press, 2007)

Replica Virginian Algonquian homes at Jamestown Settlement. (Photos: Jamestown-Yorktown Foundation)

Many Names

Indians had more than one name as they moved through life. Some names were deeply private and may have been kept secret, used only among those who shared close personal relationships. Others reflected nicknames or a station in life. As a younger man, Powhatan was known as Wahunsenacawh. He later adopted the title of Powhatan after the community in which he was born.

Some scholars believe that Werowocomoco and Orapax may have been among these districts as well. The inheritance of these relationships means that someone in Powhatan's family had been a strong leader before him.

Powhatan expanded his authority, probably through a combination of intimidation, force, spiritual and political influence, and intermarriage. In 1607, he apparently told John Smith that many groups brought him tribute. However, the nature and strength of the relationships probably varied. The English assumed that Powhatan ruled these groups like a European king, although Powhatan denied that they were under his command. The groups paid tribute to Powhatan with corn, meat, pottery, deerskins, and other gifts. In exchange, Powhatan provided them with food when needed, military or hunting assistance, and spiritual power, which he distributed in the form of copper or other spiritually imbued items.

The Indians who paid tribute to Powhatan were all based east of the fall line. The fall line is a geographical feature—a rise in elevation between the coastal and piedmont plains, which creates waterfalls in the rivers and makes it difficult to move upstream by boat. The fall line lays between the more westerly, upstream Indians who were primarily Siouan-speaking, including the Monacan, and the Algonquian-speaking people who lived to the east. These groups met at the fall line to trade, and men from both sides repeatedly crossed it on raids. Today, travelers on Interstate 95 roughly follow the fall line as it passes through Virginia and Maryland.

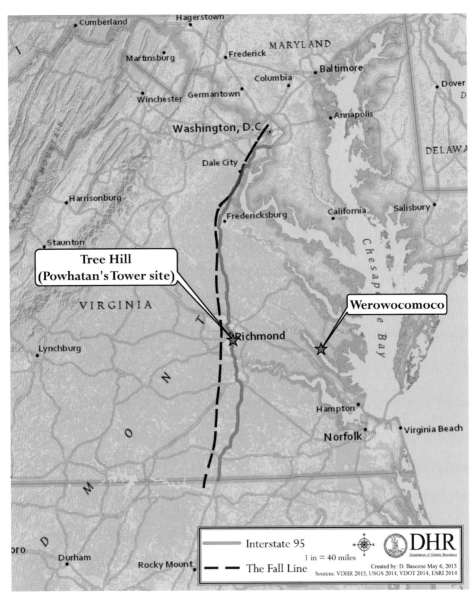

Interstate 95 through Virginia mostly parallels the geographic feature known as the fall line. Tree Hill, today a privately owned property east of Richmond, is believed to be the location of Powhatan's Tower, the settlement along the present-day James River where Wahunsenacawh (paramount chief Powhatan) lived during childhood. (VDHR)

Rapids on the Rappahannock River, near Fredericksburg, occur at the fall line, where the river passes from the harder bedrock of the upper Piedmont plain to the lower, softer sedimentary bedrock of the coastal plain. (Photo: Joe Betts)

John Smith's "Map of Virginia," published in 1612, depicts more than a hundred Indian communities living along the rivers of Tidewater Virginia. Powhatan resided on the shores of the Paumaunke (now York) River in the district of Werowocomoco. Other groups shared names with their settlements and local rivers. Among them were the Nansemond, Mattaponi, Rappahannock, and Chickahominy. The Chickahominy Indians, living southwest of Werowocomoco along the Chickahominy River, were a large group with many towns, governed by a council of elders. The Chickahominy were said to have made occasional gifts to Powhatan and allied with him at times, but did not pay regular tribute and remained independent of his influence.

Following pages: *Map of Virginia by Captain John Smith, published in 1612. Smith and his explorers found hundreds of American Indian settlements along the rivers and bays of Virginia, including Werowocomoco (see page 5 for a map detail showing Werowocomoco.). American Indian towns or settlements could shift location over time. The territories in between settlements were porous, as were the areas between tribes which were used by all people. (Library of Congress)*

POWHATAN

Held this state & fashion when Capt. Smith was deliuered to him prisoner 1607

Smith's map also shows native groups beyond Powhatan's direct influence. Along what is now called the Potomac River, the Patawomeck appear to have had some alliance with Powhatan, but the exact relationship is unclear and may have changed over time. To the south were the Chowan and Mangoag, who were not known to pay tribute to Powhatan. Upstream and to the west, the Mannahoac lived along the Rappahannock River, and the Monacan lived along the Powhatan (now James) River. Colonial sources also recorded encounters with an inland group known as the Massawomeck, who were said to be far-ranging and fearsome raiders from the North. The Susquehannock lived above the falls of the Susquehanna River in present-day Pennsylvania. The Tockwagh and Kuskarawaok, later known as Nanticoke, lived on the Chesapeake Bay's Eastern Shore.

Indians on the Chesapeake's coastal plain apparently began organizing into larger communities by the 1500s. Some historians and archeologists suggest that this was a reaction to the colonial incursions of Spain and England. Others believe that tension with Indian groups to the west and the north may have triggered a change, along with similar conflicts among groups within Virginia's Coastal Plain itself. Although there is no historical or archeological record to support the possibility, such conflicts might have occurred relatively often, while early contact with Europeans was less frequent. In fact, documented encounters between the Spanish and English with Indians in what is now Virginia and North Carolina occurred only once or twice a decade between 1560 and 1607. Although great change was on the horizon, driven by forces across the sea, the intrusion of Europeans into the Chesapeake Bay was only one of many factors at play.

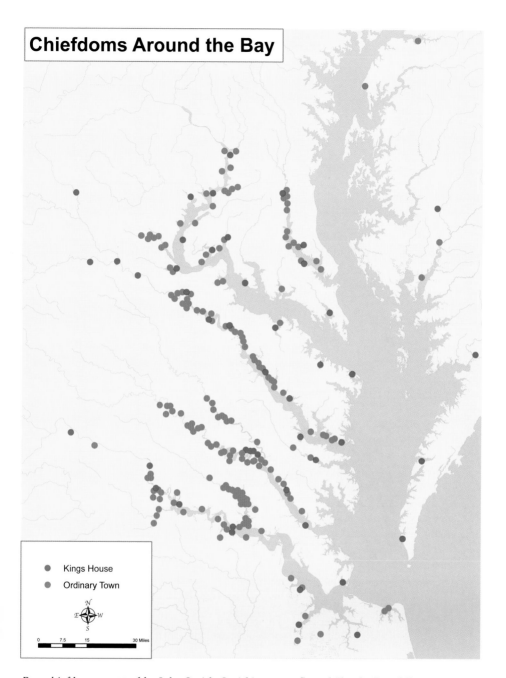

Chiefdoms Around the Bay

Bay chiefdoms mapped by John Smith. Smith's map reflected "leader" and "commoner" settlements during the period 1607–1609 and has proven an invaluable tool for scholars attempting to understand the complex and diverse native cultures of the Bay. (Map and caption adapted from John Smith's Chesapeake Voyages 1607–1609)

Chapter 4
Werowocomoco in the Written Record

Lynn and Bob Ripley began living on the shores of the York River in Gloucester County, Virginia, in 1996. Their home is situated on more than 300 acres. Some of the land has been cleared for a yard and some is covered by trees. At the time, the Ripleys also leased land to local farmers, who grew corn, beans, and wheat. Lynn Ripley loved to roam over all of it. On the fields where the earth was turned for planting and along the shoreline where water eroded the bank, she began to spot things that looked out of place. Although she didn't know it at the time, the fragments of pottery, stone tools, and projectile points she collected would later be considered the first pieces of Werowocomoco history likely held by human hands in at least 400 years.

Until then, anyone interested in Werowocomoco could only draw on oral traditions, early maps, and the written words of European colonists, mostly English men, who described what they saw or heard from others during the early 1600s. As important as these written records are, the journals, letters, and community records of that time are filled with the bias and limitations of European perspectives.

Lynn Ripley participating in archeological investigations at Werowocomoco during a 2003 summer research season under the direction of the Werowocomoco Research Group and the College of William and Mary with support from the Virginia Department of Historic Resources. (Photo: Bob Ripley)

First Spain and then England claimed the area as their own before they knew much about the land, let alone the people who lived there. They aimed to profit from the resources they found. The Jamestown colony, a project of the Virginia Company of London, was a corporate venture with stockholders, and the English had strategic reasons for gathering information about the land and its people. As newcomers, English colonists tended to flatten or simplify their interpretations of the behavior and practices they encountered, and they missed or misunderstood important parts of the picture.

Captain John Smith, a leader at James Fort between 1607 and 1609, appears to have been the first person from the settlement to set foot in Werowocomoco and meet Powhatan, whom he saw as an emperor or king.

Smith's accounts are detailed and well known, including his acquaintance with Powhatan's young daughter Pocahontas. Smith first wrote about these events in 1608, close to the time they happened, and again in the decades that followed. The details, and sometimes the stories themselves, are different in each account.

NOVA BRITANNIA.

OFFERING MOST

Excellent fruites by Planting in VIRGINIA.

Exciting all such as be well affected to further the same.

LONDON
Printed for SAMVEL MACHAM, and are to besold at his Shop in Pauls Church-yard, at the Signe of the Bul-head.
1609.

This publication written by Robert Gray, a London preacher, encourages people of England to emigrate to Virginia. It was published in 1609. (Virginia Historical Society)

His records of conversations with Powhatan Indians are surprisingly elaborate for someone who had little knowledge of their language and was at times working without any translator by his side.

Smith was observant, skilled, and curious, but he also liked to promote himself as a bold hero and man of action. As a result, historians suspect that some of his stories are exaggerated or entirely invented. His accounts of Pocahontas have been debated for just this reason. Smith's *Generall Historie of Virginia, New-England, and the Summer Isles* was published in 1624, 17 years after he first visited Werowocomoco. In this book, Smith relates a dramatic story in which Pocahontas saves him from execution while he was a captive at Werowocomoco. However, he makes no mention of this rescue in his 1608 writings from Jamestown. The scene is similar to Smith's accounts of his time in Eastern Europe and the Ottoman Empire during the late 1500s in which he describes other instances in which young women saved him from peril. While Pocahontas did play a notable part in the contact between cultures, some scholars believe that the rescue story is pure myth.

Smith's records consistently say that he found himself in Werowocomoco in 1607 because he was captured and taken there. The colonists had been at James Fort for nearly seven months, and they were barely holding on. Nearly half of the original colonists were dead from starvation, disease, and conflicts with the Indians.

An engraving depicting John Smith. (Jamestown-Yorktown Foundation collections)

Cover of John Smith's Generall Historie of Virginia, New-England, and the Summer Isles, *published in 1624, 17 years after Smith first visited Werowocomoco. (Library of Congress)*

Powhatan apparently heard of the colony's struggles to acquire food from Indians closer to the fort, and he sent gifts of corn and other provisions at strategic moments that kept at least some of the colonists from starvation. He received copper objects, glass beads, and iron hatchets in return. Powhatan sent emissaries; he did not visit James Fort himself.

Smith had been placed in charge of relations with the Indians shortly before his capture. On December 10, he took nine men in a shallop five miles up the Powhatan (now James) River. They entered the mouth of the Chickahominy River, where they passed a series of settlements and the densely populated Moysonec peninsula.

At the town of Apocant, the Chickahominy became too narrow for the shallop. Indian guides agreed to lead Smith and two others upriver in a canoe, while the rest of the crew waited with the shallop.

The next day, Smith's group came under attack. His English companions were killed, and Smith was captured by a hunting party led by Powhatan's military leader, Opechancanough. Surrounded by a large group of men—which he later was told included Pamunkey, Mattaponi, Paspahegh, Chickahominy, Chiskiack, and Youghtanund—Smith was taken captive and held for about four weeks. Opechancanough took Smith to several Indian towns before presenting him to Powhatan. Their meeting took place at Werowocomoco.

Smith said he was met by 200 "courtiers," who studied him closely. Powhatan then received Smith in his longhouse. Smith describes the scene in *A True Relation of Virginia*, published in 1608.

This Sidney E. King (1906-2002) painting depicts Jamestown settlers trading with Powhatan Indians. The English needed food from the natives in order to survive, while the Powhatans sought the colonists' commercial goods, such as metal tools, glass beads, and copper. Exchanges could be forceful or friendly. The Powhatans sometimes offered corn as a gift; at other times, they refused contact, or attacked those who had come to trade. The English wrote home of successful trading, yet on occasion they stole or raided at gunpoint. (National Park Service, Colonial National Historical Park, Jamestown collection)

Arriving at Werowocomoco, their emperor proudly lying upon a Bedstead a foote high upon tenne or twelve Mattes, richly hung with manie Chanynes of great Pearles about his necke, and covered with a great Covering of rahoughcums [raccoons]: At his heade sat a woman, at his feete another, on each side sitting uppon a Matte upon the ground were raunged his chiefe men on each side the fire, tenne in a ranke, and behind them as many yong women, each a great Chaine of white Beades over their shoulders, their heads painted in redde, [he] with such a grave and Majesticall countenance.

In this 1608 account, Smith reported that a series of feasts and conversations then took place between Powhatan and his captive. Powhatan asked why the colonists had come. Smith lied, claiming they had been driven to the area by Spanish enemies, bad weather, and damaged vessels. Powhatan described the coastal region and the people within and around these domains. Smith in turn described Europe and Captain Christopher Newport, who supervised the James Fort settlement.

Powhatan said that the English should leave James Fort and move closer to Werowocomoco. They should also provide hatchets and copper. If they followed these instructions, Powhatan would feed and protect them. Powhatan's offer suggests that he saw the English as potential allies.

Smith's *Generall Historie*, published in 1624, added the story of his rescue by Pocahontas. Smith wrote that, after a long discussion, "two great stones were brought before Powhatan" and Smith's head was pushed down on top of them. As he was surrounded by men "ready with their clubs, to beate out his braines," Pocahontas stepped forward to protest. And then, according to Smith, "Pocahontas the Kings dearest daughter, when no intreaty could prevaile, got his head in her armes, and laid her owne upon his to save him from death." Smith and other colonists described Pocahontas as about ten years old at

This detail from the Hondius-Blaeu Map of Virginia, circa 1630, depicts Powhatan seated in his lodge at Werowocomoco. The image is a colorized version of the original drawing in John Smith's Map of 1612, and it evokes Smith's description of his meeting with Powhatan, as relayed in the 1608 publication, A True Relation of Virginia. *(Jamestown-Yorktown Foundation)*

STATVS REGIS POWHATAN
quando prefectus Smith Captivus) Appomatuck
illi daretur

the time of these events. By the time Smith published this story in 1624, both Pocahontas and Powhatan had died.

If this rescue scene, or some version of it, actually happened, some scholars believe it may have been part of an "adoption" ceremony rather than an execution—representing Smith's symbolic death and rebirth as part of the Powhatan chiefdom. Also in his 1624 work, Smith describes another exchange that some scholars say suggests an "adoption" ceremony. Two days before his release, Smith was taken to a structure in the woods at Werowocomoco and placed before a fire. Powhatan appeared with a large group of Indians, all painted in black. Powhatan approached Smith, promising friendship and requesting cannons and a grindstone. According to Smith, Powhatan declared that he would "for ever esteeme him as his sonne Nantaquod." Smith was then released and he returned to James Fort. While adopting Smith could have been a strategic move on Powhatan's part, no evidence of this kind of ritual has yet been uncovered among other Algonquian-speaking peoples.

Smith describes traveling to Werowocomoco to meet with Powhatan four more times: three times in 1608 and once in 1609. His first return trip came about one month after his release, when Powhatan wanted to meet Captain Newport. Smith and Newport, along with 30 to 40 men, sailed to Powhatan's headquarters. When they arrived, Smith took 20 armed men into Werowocomoco while Newport remained with the boat. Smith described his approach to the town, which rose along a small bay fed by three creeks, all within a mile of each other. The bay, he wrote, was "all ooze." They found themselves mistakenly on one of the creeks instead of the bay, and a man Smith described as Powhatan's son helped escort them into town.

Smith presented Powhatan with gifts of cloth, a hat, and a dog. The exchange was friendly, but Smith was cautious. He did not allow his men to put down their weapons or to enter a longhouse alone. Smith offered to help fight the Monacan to the west and the "Pocoughtaonack," possibly the Susquehannock, to the north. According to Smith, Powhatan was pleased.

A modern statue of Christopher Newport, located at the entrance to Christopher Newport University in Newport News, Virginia. The Virginia Company of London appointed Newport, a privateer and ship captain, leader of the 1606 voyage from England that resulted in the founding of Jamestown in 1607. The statue has been criticized by some historians for inaccurately depicting Newport with two arms, since he lost one to an infected battle wound he received years before voyaging to North America. (Photo: VDHR)

Powhatan declared Smith a werowance and the James Fort settlement part of Powhatan's chiefdom. As such, the colonists would be allowed to have corn, women, and land.

The next day, Powhatan took Smith to the river. Powhatan pointed to his canoes and described the system of tribute through which he received food, deerskins, and other gifts. A short while later, Newport came ashore. When the two leaders met, Powhatan again asked the colonists to lay down their arms. As a compromise, Newport sent his men back to the waterline. Smith was not happy—the considerable distance between Powhatan's longhouse and the river made them vulnerable to attack.

The colonists stayed at Werowocomoco for several days. They exchanged hatchets, copper pots, and blue beads for bushels of corn. The colonists saw this as trade. Powhatan may have seen it as an exchange of gifts. In any case, the Indians showed strong interest in the blue beads, which some scholars suggest were seen as objects of spiritual power. The English interrupted their stay at Werowocomoco to visit Opechancanough at the town of Pamunkey, where the exchange of food and goods also centered on blue beads.

Later in 1608, during the fall, the Virginia Company of London sent special instructions to the colonists. They were asked to crown Powhatan and make him a vassal to King James of England. Newport agreed. Smith thought it was a waste of time, but traveled to Werowocomoco to invite Powhatan to the fort, where the English hoped to conduct the coronation. Powhatan was away when Smith arrived. While waiting for his return, Smith was brought to a field and placed before a fire. Soon a group of about 30 warriors ran into the field, vocalizing loudly. Assuming he was under attack, Smith prepared to defend himself. In one version of Smith's accounts, Pocahontas appeared and explained that no harm was intended. Smith noticed that men, women, and children were among the group that was forming, and he let down his guard. Women formed a ring around the fire and began to dance and sing. They were clothed in leaves and adorned with white, red, and

Glass beads recovered by archeologists at the site of Jordan's Journey, a 1619 English settlement on the south side of the James River, just east of present-day Hopewell. The site is on a prominent peninsula, now known as Jordan's Point, occupied by American Indians prior to 1619. It was one of the earliest English settlements after Jamestown. Similar beads were recovered at Werowocomoco. (Photos: VDHR)

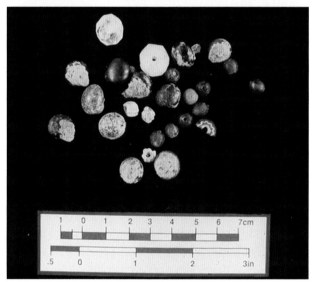

black paint. The group's leader wore deer antlers on her head while others carried bows and arrows, clubs, and swords. After an hour of impassioned and solemn performance, the women made an exit into the woods.

The next day, Powhatan arrived. Smith again offered presents and assistance in attacking the Monacan, which Powhatan replied he did not need. Powhatan also said that Newport should come to Werowocomoco to bring his presents, and Smith returned to James Fort with the message. The English did as Powhatan asked, and the crowning took place at Werowocomoco. During a ceremony that must have been strange for all involved, Newport presented gifts to Powhatan, including a pitcher, a basin, a bed, and a red cloak. But Powhatan resisted the crowning. Smith wrote:

> *A foule trouble there was to make him kneele to receive his Crowne, he neither knowing the majesty nor meaning of a Crowne, nor bending of the knee, endured so many perswasions, examples, and instructions, as tyred them all; at last by leaning hard on his shoulders, he a little stooped, and three having the crowne in their hands put it on his head, when by the warning of a Pistoll the Boats were prepared with such a volley of shot, that the King start up in a horrible feare, till he saw all was well.*

Powhatan then gave his shoes and a mantle to Newport, along with seven or eight bushels of corn.

A few months later, the situation for the colony had taken a turn for the worse. Winter had arrived, and the Indians had stopped trading with the colonists. The English assumed that this was on Powhatan's orders. In desperation, Smith led a party to a Nansemond town. They took a large quantity of corn by firing muskets, burning a house, and threatening to burn the entire community. They considered attacking Werowocomoco, too.

In December 1608, Powhatan sent word that he would help feed the colonists if they would build an English-style house for him at Werowocomoco. He also wanted a grindstone, 50 swords, guns, a rooster, a hen, copper, and beads. The leaders at James Fort agreed to all but the swords and guns. They sent about 20 men to help build the house, partially because they believed it would help them stage a surprise attack.

In January 1609, Smith paid another visit to Werowocomoco. It would be his last. Powhatan was reluctant to provide the corn he had promised, and Smith would not make gifts of guns or swords. The situation was especially tense because Powhatan knew about the attack on the Nansemond. Also, some of the colonists who were sent to build Powhatan's house may have offered more truthful insights regarding the Virginia Company and its intent to colonize the area. Powhatan's words, as Smith describes them, are moving:

> *Some doubt I have of your comming hither, that makes me not so kindly seeke to relieve you as I would: for many doe informe me, your comming hither is not for trade, but to invade my people, and possesse my Country. . . . To free us of this feare, leave aboard your weapons, for here they are needlesse, we being all friends, and for ever Powhatans.*

Powhatan eventually exchanged corn for a copper kettle. Smith's account of his speech continues:

> *You may understand that I having seene the death of all my people thrice, and not anyone living of these three generations but my selfe; I know the difference of Peace and Warre better than any in my Country. . . . What will it availe you to take that by force you may quickly have by love, or to destroy them that provide you food. What can you get by warre, when we can hide our provisions and fly to the woods? Whereby you must famish by wronging us your friends.*

The rest of the visit was tense. Both Indians and English expected an ambush. Cocking their weapons, the colonists convinced the Indians to carry the corn to the barges waiting along the shore. The colonists then waited in Werowocomoco until the tide rose and the barges could float free of the half-frozen marsh.

This was Smith's last description of Werowocomoco. Shortly after he left, two German colonists who had been sent to build the house for Powhatan returned to James Fort while Smith was still traveling. They claimed, falsely, that Smith had asked them to bring weapons to Werowocomoco. The fort leadership gave them the weapons. The day after they departed for Werowocomoco, several other colonists decided to abandon the misery of James Fort for refuge with the Indians. Six or seven men stole swords, pike heads, firearms, shot, and powder when they left.

This engraving, the earliest image of Pocahontas, was published in Smith's The Historie of Virginia, New-England, and the Summer Isles *(1624). It shows her as the wife of John Rolfe and was made in 1616 when she was in England, where she died in 1617. By the time she traveled to England, she had taken the Christian name of Rebecca. "The sponsors of the Jamestown colony saw marketing possibilities in the regal, converted, English-speaking princess,"* John F. Ross *wrote in* Smithsonian *magazine about this image. "Luring new colonists to Jamestown and finding investors for the venture was a hard sell. What better 'poster girl' than Pocahontas?" (Library of Congress)*

Pocahontas, a daughter of Powhatan, was living at Werowocomoco and visited James Fort during the early years of the English settlement. According to Captain John Smith, Pocahontas was about 10 years old when the English established the fort in 1607. Powhatan had many children, but Pocahontas was said to be his favorite. Stories suggest she was bright, curious, and playful. As a young woman Pocahontas revealed on two occasions that she was also known as Matoaka; her childhood name was reported to have been Amonute.

Smith described her as the chief's "litle Daughter" and "a child of tenne years old." Smith said Pocahontas stood out for her "feature, countenance, and proportion" and was "for wit, and spirit, the only Nonpareil of his Country." Pocahontas visited James Fort several times. On her first visit, she came with one of her father's councillors to negotiate the release of Indian prisoners. She also accompanied the Indians who brought food to the starving colonists. She was said to have turned cartwheels with the boys of the fort wearing little clothing, an indication that she was still too young to dress as a woman at the time. Some scholars suggest that her presence was useful to the Indians as an observer of conditions in James Fort.

In 1624, Smith published accounts about Pocahontas that didn't appear in any of his earlier writings. In them, Pocahontas saved Smith's life on at least two occasions. She first begged Powhatan to spare Smith's life when he was a captive at Werowocomoco. Later, she warned Smith and his men about plans to ambush and poison them.

Some scholars question whether these accounts are true, but the rescue stories have inspired many creative tales about Pocahontas; a number of them were written during the early years of the United States, when accounts of "good Indians" were popular. Some of these tales portray Pocahontas as a young woman in a romance with John Smith, but there is no evidence of a romantic relationship between them. She was a still a child when he was in Virginia.

As a young teenager, Pocahontas reportedly married an Indian named Kocoum. Nothing more is known of him. In March 1613, at the age of 15 or 16, Pocahontas was kidnapped by the English. Captain Samuel Argall hoped to ransom her for the return of English prisoners and weapons, but Powhatan did not respond. While a captive, Pocahontas was taught about English religion and how to behave as an Englishwoman. She also met a widower, John Rolfe, who wished to marry her.

Powhatan eventually agreed to the marriage. Pocahontas formally adopted Christianity and a new name, Rebecca. She and Rolfe wed in 1614 and had a son named Thomas. Their marriage preceded several years of peace between the Indians and the colonists.

The Virginia Company of London decided that taking the "civilized" Pocahontas to England would help recruit more support for the Virginia Colony. In 1616, the company took Pocahontas, Rolfe, and their young son, Thomas, across the Atlantic for a tour of England. While there, Pocahontas met John Smith one last time.

Pocahontas died in England of an unknown illness in March 1617, just before her return to Virginia. She was about 20 years old when she died. Her husband returned to Virginia, leaving their young son to be raised by the Rolfe family in England.

An engraving based on an 1855 painting titled "The Marriage of Pocahontas" by Henry Brueckner was widely distributed in the mid-19th century in the U.S. and Europe. There is no evidence that there was ever a romantic relationship between John Smith and Pocahontas, who was around 10 years old when the two first met. She did, however, later marry Jamestown colonist John Rolfe. (Virginia Historical Society)

A delegation of Virginia Indians journeyed to England in July, 2006. Their agenda included a visit to Gravesend, in Kent, where Pocahontas is believed to be buried underneath the chancel of the parish church of St. George. When she died, Pocahontas (Rebecca) was in England with her husband, John Rolfe, and their two-year-old son Thomas. She was returning to the Virginia Colony when she became ill and died in 1617. Her exact resting place is unknown because a 1727 fire burned the earlier church. The statue of Pocahontas silhouetted here is a duplicate of the one at Historic Jamestown. (Photo: VDHR)

A statue of Pocahontas at Historic Jamestown, Virginia. (Photo: VDHR)

The winter of 1609–1610 was known at Jamestown as the "Starving Time," when more than 80 percent of the 500 colonists perished. This painting by Sidney E. King is titled "Burial of the Dead, 1609–10." (National Park Service, Colonial National Historical Park, Jamestown collection)

In the meantime, Smith was attempting to trade for corn at Pamunkey. The visit went badly. Growing distrust between Indians and colonists led to more conflicts. Smith reported at least two attempts on his life. At one point, he seized Opechancanough and threatened to shoot him. Smith then led raids along the Pamunkey and Mattaponi rivers. As he returned downstream, he neared Werowocomoco. Smith sent scouts ahead of him, and they returned with surprising news. Powhatan had moved to the town of Orapax, to the west on the Chickahominy River. Werowocomoco was never mentioned in English records again.

Chapter 5
Return to Werowocomoco

When Powhatan left Werowocomoco and made his new headquarters at Orapax, on the upper reaches of the Chickahominy River, Indian dealings with the English were far from over. The land known as Werowocomoco, however, was lost in the relentless march of English settlement. Before long, its exact location was unclear. Werowocomoco became more of a story than a place. The next pivotal chapter would begin nearly 400 years later, in Bob and Lynn Ripley's garage.

In 2001, Fairfield Foundation archeologists David Brown and Thane Harpole met with the Ripleys while talking with Gloucester County landowners about the results of an archeological survey that had taken place in the county during the 1970s. Brown and Harpole were already thinking of Werowocomoco when they arrived. They knew that Randolph Turner, an archeologist and expert on the Powhatan era at the Virginia Department of Historic Resources, had long suspected that this property could be the site of Werowocomoco, and he was not the first archeologist to do so. Shortly before their meeting with the Ripleys, a neighbor mentioned that Lynn Ripley had found a large number of artifacts on the property.

She was happy to show them her collection, and the archeologists were stunned by what they saw. The Ripleys had converted their garage into a storage and workspace for the pieces she had found. Lynn Ripley had carefully sorted hundreds of artifacts, most of which had been found along the eroding shoreline. Some were from the 1700s, and some dated to more recent decades. But most were Indian projectile points, stone flakes, and pieces of native pottery. "We explained that, if this site was near Werowocomoco, you would expect to find a lot of small triangular points, which were common in the Late Woodland Period," Harpole said. "Then Lynn brought out a whole pan full."

In 2008, the Virginia Department of Historic Resources approved a state historical marker highlighting Orapax. The marker reads: "Powhatan, the paramount chief of many Virginia Algonquian tribes when the English first landed at Jamestown, lived near here at the town of Orapax, having moved from Werowocomoco in 1609 following conflicts with the English. The English boy Henry Spelman lived with Powhatan at Orapax for several months during 1609. By 1614, Powhatan had moved again to Matchcot on the Pamunkey River. In Captain John Smith's 1624 writings, Smith recounted that he had been taken to Orapax after being captured near the Chickahominy River in 1607 by men of several tribes who were under the leadership of Opechancanough, Powhatan's military leader." (Photo: VDHR)

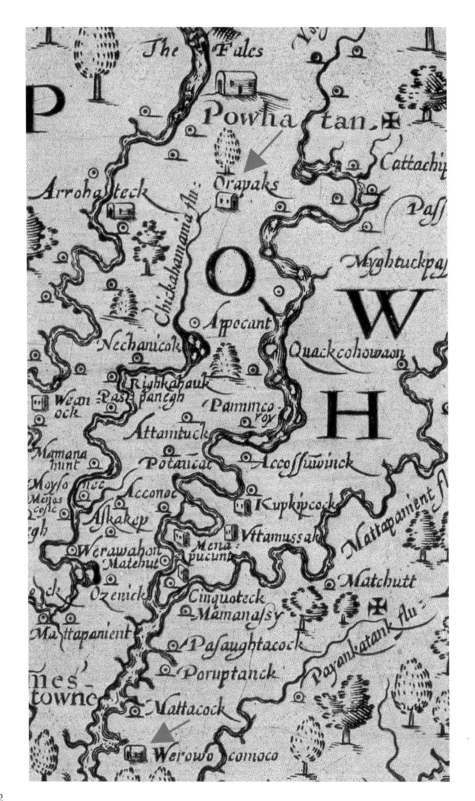

Small bits of copper caught Brown and Harpole's trained eyes. These pieces were not of Indian origin. The Ripleys thought they might date to the Civil War, but Brown and Harpole suspected otherwise. It looked like metal that could have arrived here much earlier—possibly in the hands of John Smith when he was trading with Powhatan. "We realized right away that those materials were not from the Civil War," Brown said. "Most likely, they were from the time of European contact."

A mixture of Indian and European artifacts could be expected at a number of Indian sites that date to the early 1600s. But Brown and Harpole quickly associated the artifacts they saw with Werowocomoco because clues to Werowocomoco's location already pointed to Purtan Bay. Along with the written descriptions by Smith and other colonists, scholars have used three maps to support this conclusion.

Two examples of copper pieces that caught the eyes of archeologists Thane Harpole and Dr. David Brown of the Fairfield Foundation. (Photo: WRG)

Opposite: *In 1609 Powhatan departed Werowocomoco and relocated with his people at the settlement of Orapax along the Chickahominy River in present-day New Kent County, Virginia. This excerpt from the John Smith Map of Virginia (1612) shows Orapax (top arrow) in relation to Werowocomoco (bottom arrow). "The Fales [Falls]" indicated at the very top of the map is the site of present-day Richmond. (VDHR)*

The Plow Zone

Lynn Ripley found artifacts near the surface of the land because plowing had turned up the soil and pulled them to the top. The plow zone—the depth to which a plow disturbs the soil—is usually about 12 inches deep.

Artifacts in the plow zone have been dislodged from their original location and depth in the earth, and from the features where they were deposited, such as pits and ditches. But the objects generally do not move far from their original position and can indicate locations worthy of close study. To conduct a thorough investigation, archeologists excavate the plow zone and carefully examine the layers of soil beneath it.

Plow zone artifacts still provide important information about a site, so it is best for nonprofessionals to leave artifacts where they lie and report their finds to a museum or archeologist. At Werowocomoco, plow zone artifacts were among the clues that helped archeologists plan targeted excavations across a 50-acre site.

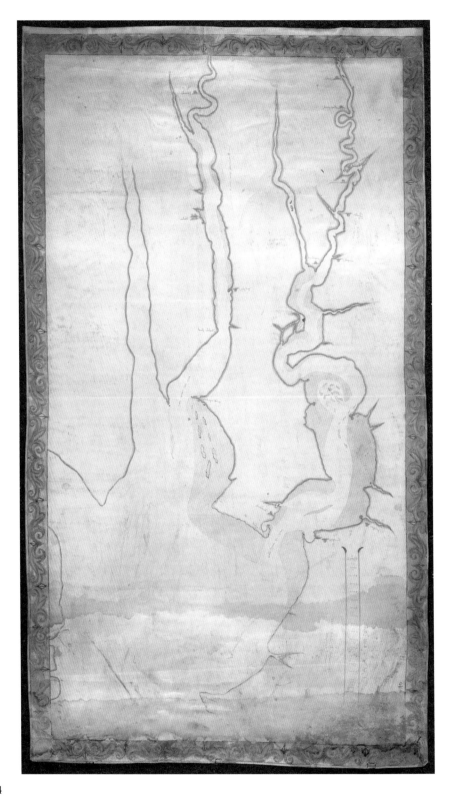

The 1608 map by Robert Tindall, one of Jamestown's original colonists, is hand-drawn. Tindall marked the village of "Poetan" on the shore of what is now the York River with a drawing of four native houses. Most researchers agree that "Poetan" is likely Tindall's name for Werowocomoco, given that the town was known primarily as Powhatan's residence and Tindall was among those who visited Werowocomoco in person. The shape of the shoreline at Poetan suggests a small bay fed by three streams; Purtan Bay is fed by three creeks, now named Purtan, Leigh, and Bland. Tindall's map also marks the location of Chiskiack, downstream from Poetan on the opposite shore. This matches the locations of the site now identified as Werowocomoco and the location of the site of Chiskiack, which researchers identified in 2003 on the grounds of the Naval Weapons Station in York County.

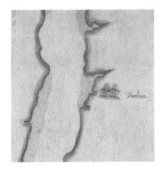

Robert Tindall's map of 1608 shows the settlement of "Poetan" (Werowocomoco) with a drawing of four native houses (detail). Significantly the map suggests the settlement is along a bay in the York River and also indicates that three creeks empty into the bay. Tindall was among the very few Europeans who actually visited Werowocomoco. (British Library Board. Source: Cotton Augustus I. ii. 46)

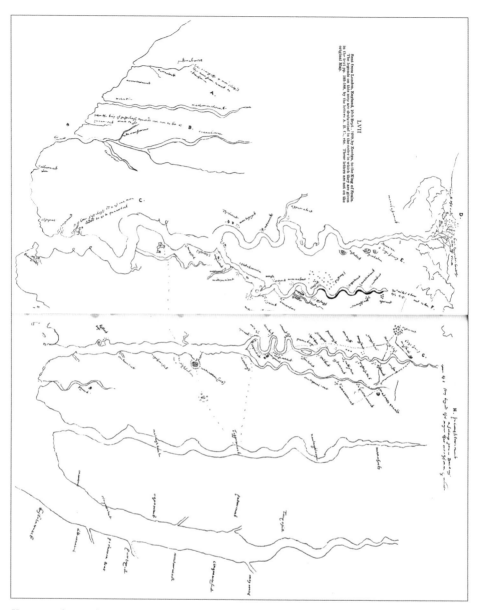

Known today as the Zuñiga Chart, this map (slightly enhanced here for legibility) accompanied a 1608 letter from Don Pedro de Zuñiga to King Philip II of Spain that reported on activities of the English at Jamestown. The map appears to be a copy of a sketch that Capt. John Smith sent to England with his manuscript of A True Relation of Virginia *in 1608. (From* The Genesis of the United States *by Alexander Brown. Boston: Houghton, Mifflin and Company, 1890)*

This detail from the Zuñiga Chart shows James Fort (Jamestown), indicated in the lower left by a triangular symbol. Werowocomoco, on the right, is represented with a symbol similar in shape to the letter D inside a circle of dots and is comparable in size to the James Fort triangle, conveying the strategic importance of Powhatan's settlement. The map's dotted line marks the route that Smith traveled during his captivity. (WRG)

Smith's Map of Virginia was published in 1612 as an artistic, printed document in a formal mapmaking style. On this map, Werowocomoco is depicted as 14 miles upstream from Tyndall's Point and 9 miles above Chiskiack. It is also 11 miles below the confluence of the Pamunkey River (labeled on the map as the Youghtanund) and the Mattaponi. These distances closely match those on the Tindall map. The shoreline again includes a small bay and indentations that suggest three creeks.

The third map is a hand-drawn image that was discovered in a Spanish archive. This map accompanied a 1608 letter from Don Pedro de Zuñiga to King Philip II of Spain, informing the king about developments in the English colony. The Zuñiga map appears to be a copy of a sketch that Smith sent to England with his manuscript of *A True Relation* of *Virginia in 1608*. The Zuñiga map marks locations of more than 60 Indian communities, the triangular shape of James Fort, and the route Smith traveled during his captivity.

Crumbling Shorelines and Rising Water

A breakwater of stone erected along the shoreline at Werowocomoco offers some protection to its vulnerable riverbank, slowing the pace of erosion, a problem that will be addressed in the future with construction of a more substantial breakwater. (Photos: Bob Ripley)

Shorelines throughout the Chesapeake Bay region are steadily washing away. Two forces are at work—erosion and a rising sea level. As a result, shorelines have crumbled, and land where people once lived has sunk beneath the waves. The process sometimes reveals clues to the past that would otherwise be hidden in the soil, and it helped Lynn Ripley  spot native artifacts along the shoreline at Werowocomoco.

Archeologists and scientists worry that valuable sites will be lost to the water faster than they can be studied. Parts of Werowocomoco have already eroded into the water. It was long believed that the remains of James Fort were underwater, too, but archeologists confirmed in 1996 that all but one corner of the original site is still on dry land and accessible for research.

Werowocomoco is marked on the shore of a small, defined bay upstream from Chiskiack. At Werowocomoco, there is an unusual symbol. Its shape is similar to two capital letter D's that overlap slightly, like a blurred double image. A series of dots surround it. The meaning of the symbol is not marked on the map, but its size is easily comparable to James Fort and appears to convey the site's strategic importance.

Despite speculations about Purtan Bay as the possible location of Werowocomoco, the property was not officially noted in Virginia's archeological inventory until 1977. It was then that Daniel Mouer, an archeologist with Virginia Commonwealth University, paid a visit. He found Indian artifacts on what later became the Ripleys' property and identified the land as the possible location of Werowocomoco. This was the last professional attention directed at the site until 2001, when David Brown and Thane Harpole asked Randolph Turner to assess Lynn Ripley's artifacts.

Turner, an expert on the archeology of the Powhatan era, had been intrigued by the Purtan Bay site early in his career. In the 1970s, he visited Gloucester County to work on his doctoral dissertation and stopped by the property. "I traveled down that gravel road several times, but the owners were never home," Turner said. Now, decades later, the land had new owners. The Ripleys were not only home, but eager to help.

The timing could not have been better. The 400th anniversary of the Jamestown settlement was just six years away. Partners in Virginia and throughout the Chesapeake region were making plans to commemorate the founding of James Fort, Smith's exploration of the Chesapeake Bay, and English interactions with Virginia Indians. Their work was propelled by the archeological discovery of James Fort itself, which was announced in 1996. Yet there was no major project related to Virginia Indians that could help balance perspectives on the historic events of the early 1600s. American Indians in Virginia had always cared about their heritage, but the added interest of the general public, academic community, and media was about to reach a peak.

Werowocomoco After 1609

After the Indians left Werowocomoco, the land played host to a small collection of families—the Taliaferros, Caffees, Blands, and Stubblefields—who farmed the fields, harvested timber, and created the rural landscape seen today. Indians, historians, and archeologists continued to associate Werowocomoco with the north shore of the York River, but its exact location was disputed. About 10 miles downstream from Purtan Bay, an area of Gloucester County took the name of Wicomico, where an old chimney was once thought to be the remains of a house that the English agreed to build for Powhatan. The chimney still stands, but historical and archeological research has shown that it was built much later in time. Other locations for Werowocomoco were suggested over the years, but only Purtan Bay matches historical descriptions and has yielded the corresponding archeological evidence.

Werowocomoco seen from Purtan Bay. Bland Creek is to the right. (Photo: Bob Ripley)

Located about 10 miles from Werowocomoco, this chimney, according to local legend, was believed to be the remains of a house that the English agreed to build for Powhatan. Historical and archeological research has shown that it was built much later in time. (Photo: E. R. Turner)

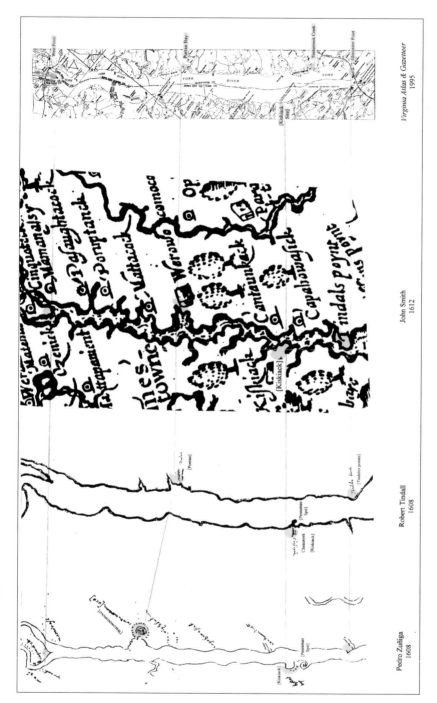

In the late 1990s, prior to the confirmation of the site through archeological "ground truthing," a historian at Virginia's Department of Historic Resources photocopied to the same scale the three historic maps of Zuñiga, Tindall, and Smith, along with a modern topographic map, to reveal the similarities among the maps in regard to the locations of Purtan Bay and Werowocomoco and other landmarks. (VDHR)

Chapter 6
The Virginia Indian Advisory Board

Archeologists David Brown and Thane Harpole conducted the first formal archeological survey of Werowocomoco in 2002. The survey, funded by the Ripleys and the Virginia Department of Historic Resources, was a sampling of the site to determine its size and research potential. Their work uncovered a concentrated array of artifacts from the Late Woodland and Mid-Atlantic Contact periods that were unmatched by earlier, informal surveys that had taken place elsewhere near Purtan Bay. In late 2002, confident that the Powhatan headquarters had indeed been identified, the Werowocomoco Research Group was formed. The team included Brown, Harpole, and Turner, as well as archeologist Martin Gallivan and cultural anthropologist Danielle Moretti-Langholtz, both with the College of William and Mary.

Members of the Werowocomoco Research Group in 2009 (L to R): Thane Harpole (Fairfield Foundation), Dr. Danielle Moretti-Langholtz (College of William and Mary), Dr. Dave Brown (Fairfield Foundation), Dr. Martin Gallivan (College of William and Mary), and Dr. Randolph Turner (Virginia Dept. of Historic Resources). (Photo: VDHR)

In February 2003, the Werowocomoco Research Group presented a detailed project proposal to chiefs and other representatives of Virginia's tribes during a meeting at the College of William and Mary.

Realizing that honoring the land and its original people was as important as any research that might take place there, the Werowocomoco Research Group sought the direct participation of Virginia Indians. "We wanted to reach out to the native community before the story became news," said Moretti-Langholtz. "Assembling a multi-tribal team of advisors to an archeological project had never been done before in Virginia but, given the historical significance of Werowocomoco, we felt it was the right approach."

As a first step, the research group met with the Virginia Council on Indians—leaders of the state-recognized tribes of Virginia—to share their findings and ask for guidance. The council, under the leadership of Reeva Tilley of the Rappahannock Tribe, expressed support and suggested creating an Indian advisory group to help with the project. In 2003, the Ripleys invited Virginia Indians to visit and tour Werowocomoco with the Werowocomoco Research Group.

Six tribes formed the Virginia Indian Advisory Board for the project. Its initial members included Jeff Brown (Pamunkey), Kerry Canaday (Chickahominy), Mark Custalow (Mattaponi), Lee Lockamy (Nansemond),

Chief Anne Richardson (Rappahannock), and the late Reggie Tupponce, Sr. (Upper Mattaponi). Ex-officio members included Chief Steve Adkins (Chickahominy), Chief Ken Adams (Upper Mattaponi), and Chief Emeritus Oliver Perry (Nansemond). Deanna Beacham, who worked for the Virginia Council on Indians, assisted the Werowocomoco Research Group during 2003.

"The members of the advisory board were not passive observers of the excavations," said Moretti-Langholtz. "They helped us frame research questions, reviewed all the technical reports, and helped us bring community members, educators, and students to the site. Their respect for the site and enthusiasm for the excavation were key factors in reaching out to their communities and the broader public."

The Virginia Indian Advisory Board worked with the research team on the procedures that would be followed if human remains were uncovered during excavations. This was an important voluntary agreement because the federally enacted American Indian Graves Protection and Repatriation Act does not apply to Virginia tribes.

Members of the Virginia Indian Advisory Board for Werowocomoco and the Werowocomoco Research Group (WRG) during an onsite meeting. (L to R): The late Reggie Tupponce, Sr. of the Upper Mattaponi; Kerry Canaday of the Chickahominy; Danielle Moretti-Langholtz of WRG and the College of William and Mary; Jeff Brown (barely visible) of the Pamunkey; Mark Custalow, Chief of the Mattaponi; Thane Harpole and (foreground) David Brown of the Fairfield Foundation; property owners Lynn Ripley (barely visible) and Bob Ripley (standing). (Photos: WRG)

May 2006. Jeff Brown (center right; red shirt and hat) stands before an excavation pit pointing out characteristics of the Werowocomoco site to staff of the Virginia Department of Historic Resources and other invited guests during a summer field school tour. Brown, an archeologist, is a Pamunkey Indian and a founding member of the Virginia Indian Advisory Board. (Photo: VDHR)

The act requires agencies and institutions that receive federal funding to return Indian cultural objects (human remains, funerary objects, sacred objects, or objects of cultural patrimony) to their associated tribes. The act applies only to tribes recognized by the federal government, however; at the time of the excavations (and at this writing), no Virginia tribe has received federal recognition. Yet the Werowocomoco Research Group wanted to follow the spirit of the legislation and included the Virginia Indian Advisory Board in establishing research questions and making decisions about the excavations.

The Ripleys invited Virginia Indians always to feel welcome at Werowocomoco. "I don't know if they believed me at first, but I meant it," Lynn Ripley said. "This is their heritage. All they have to do is call." In response to this invitation, the advisory board facilitated regular native visitation to the site, including a weeklong open house for members of the Virginia Indian community to visit the site while excavations were underway.

The Werowocomoco Research Group wanted their work to be shaped by questions that were important to the Virginia Indians. They asked members of the advisory board for their individual perspectives on the site. Many felt a powerful connection to Werowocomoco as a historic center of the Powhatan leadership and as a place for renewing the influence of Virginia Indians on representations of the native past. Others encouraged research on the influence and social complexity of the Powhatan's system of tributaries. They were less interested in Pocahontas, interactions with Europeans, and to some extent Powhatan himself. These topics had long been explored, promoted, and debated. They wanted to know more about the deep history of the site, about Werowocomoco and its people *before* Europeans arrived. How did Werowocomoco come to be? What was life like for the people who lived there? And why did Werowocomoco become a place associated with leadership and power? The land would yield some surprising answers and raise more questions, too.

Chapter 7
Werowocomoco through Archeology

When David Brown and Thane Harpole launched the first sustained archeological survey of Werowocomoco in 2002, they aimed to disturb the land as little as possible. By the end of the survey in 2003, they had completed 603 small shovel tests, each about one foot in diameter, in systematic locations across 50 acres—every 50 feet across a carefully measured grid. They screened the soil from each test pit for artifacts, then refilled the holes and covered them with a plug of grass. After several weeks of work, the fields looked as if the team had never been there. But the archeologists left with a great deal of information and the hint of more to come.

Late Woodland Indian sites identified in Virginia typically cover no more than five to ten acres of land by a watercourse. Brown and Harpole surveyed nearly 50 acres and found artifacts and features associated with native settlements across the entire site. "Everywhere we looked, there was something to be found," Brown said. Pottery and stone tools were concentrated along Purtan Bay and continued in lighter densities as far as 1,500 feet from the shore. Two small areas were found on the York River bluff that contained artifacts dating to the Middle Woodland period (approximately 500 BCE to 900 CE). Late Woodland artifacts (approximately 900 CE to 1600 CE) were located in these areas too. Four areas contained a mix of artifacts dating to the Late Woodland and Mid-Atlantic Contact periods. The two largest areas, next to the bluff above the York River, could be the residential core of the town. Fields several hundred feet from shoreline also contained notable concentrations of Late Woodland and Mid-Atlantic Contact period artifacts.

A Chronology of Virginia Indians

Time Period	Stage of Development	Cultural Period
15,000 – 8000 BCE		Paleoindian
	Early hunters	
8000 – 6000 BCE		Early Archaic
6000 – 2500 BCE		Middle Archaic
	Dispersed foragers	
2500 – 1200 BCE		Late Archaic
1200 – 500 BCE		Early Woodland
	Sedentary foragers	
500 BCE – 900 CE		Middle Woodland
900 – 1600 CE		Late Woodland
	Farmers	
1600 CE		Historic

BCE = Before Common Era (same as BC)
CE = Common Era (same as AD)

Environment	Subsistence Pattern	Social Group/ Settlement	Material Culture
Cold & moist; sedges, grasses, spruce, fir, pine	Hunting, supplemented by general gathering	Bands/ Encampments	Stone fluted points, scrapers, flake tools, wedges, gravers, drills, hammerstones
Warmer & drier: pine, spruce, fir, oak, birch, beech			Side- & corner-notched points
Warmer & moister: pine, oak, hemlock	Diversification of hunting & gathering	Band clusters/ Encampments	Atlatls, axes, pestles & mortars, net sinkers, increased use of bone scrapers and awls
Very warm & dry: oak, hickory, chestnut, pine	Intensified hunting & gathering, with introduction of ultigens (gourd & squash)	Transition to tribes/ hamlets	Soapstone vessels; shell ornaments; bone needles, pins, & fishhooks, copper artifacts Ceramic vessels & pipes Stone burial mounds, stone celts, bows & arrows
Cooler & moister: oak, chestnut, pine, hickory			
Modern conditions	Intensified hunting & gathering, with dependency on cultigens (corn, beans, squash & tobacco)	Tribes or chiefdoms/ villages	Earthen burial mounds, pictographs
	Introduction of European cultigens & domesticated animals	Population reduction, relocation & consolidation with European settlement	European ornamentation, tools & household items

– Adapted from *First People, The Early Indians of Virginia* by Keith Egloff & Deborah Woodward

Thane Harpole of the Fairfield Foundation works an excavation pit at Werowocomoco during 2003 field school. (Photo: WRG)

Overall, the distribution of artifacts suggested that Werowocomoco was the site of smaller occupations in the Middle Woodland period and during some parts of the Late Woodland period. To the archeologists, it appeared that by the late 1500s and early 1600s Werowocomoco had become a large dispersed town with a core area along the river.

In February 2003, the Werowocomoco Research Group presented a general proposal to tribal chiefs, members of the Virginia Council on Indians, and other representatives of Virginia's state-recognized tribes in meetings held at the College of William and Mary. A detailed work plan followed, created in partnership with the Virginian Indian Advisory Board, outlining several years of archeological explorations. The work took place between 2003 and 2010, supported with funds from the College of William and Mary, Virginia Department of Historic Resources, National Endowment for the Humanities, National Park Service, Virginia Foundation for the Humanities, Jamestown 400th Commemoration Commission, and Colonial Dames of America.

Dr. Dave Brown (left) of the Fairfield Foundation and James Goodwin, a student at the College of William and Mary, during a 2004 summer field school. Brown holds recovered pottery shards in his hand. (Photo: WRG)

Ashley Atkins-Spivey, a Ph.D. candidate in the department of anthropology at the College of William and Mary and a member of the Pamunkey Indian Tribe, works an excavation pit in the pasture at Werowocomoco during the 2005 summer field school. (Photo: WRG)

Support from the Ripleys was crucial. As private land-owners, the Ripleys were under no obligation to help with historical or archeological research—let alone a large, multi-year project that would dislodge earth surrounding their home, bring crews of archeology students to their land, gain the attention of state and federal officials, and draw a steady flow of reporters and film crews. The Ripleys not only tolerated this undertaking, but they also welcomed it.

The first excavations took place in June 2003, led by Martin Gallivan of the William and Mary archeological field school. David Brown and Thane Harpole served as field directors. The crew included both archeology students and Virginia Indian volunteers. Ashley Atkins-Spivey, a member of the Pamunkey Indian Tribe and anthropology student at the College of William and Mary, worked on the project for several years along with Jeff Brown, a member of the Pamunkey Tribal Council and the project's Virginia Indian Advisory Board. James Krigsvold (Pamunkey), Ethan Brown (Pamunkey), and Gloria Custalow (Mattaponi), also

Jeff Brown and a student work along the York River bluff during the 2005 field school. (Photos: WRG)

Pottery

Archeologists can find extraordinary clues in the remnants of pottery, once the objects of ordinary life.

Pottery is valuable to archeological research, in part because it is very durable. Even when broken, it lasts a long time in the archeological record. Analyzing pottery is therefore one of the most reliable ways to date the occupation of a site.

The quantity, material, style, and markings on the pottery can reveal a great deal more. If archeologists find a large number of pottery pieces in one area, they have reason to believe it was a domestic space where people were cooking and storing food. The shape of the vessels can reveal the types of activities taking place there, such as cooking, storing food, or feasting. If pottery made by different groups is found at the same location, archeologists can begin to trace interactions among them, which may have been shaped by trade or intermarriage.

Rappahannock Fabric-impressed pottery (top) and Rappahannock incised ceramics found at Werowocomoco. The latter potshards were uncovered along a riverfront excavation pit, the former in a pasture excavation pit. (Photos: VDHR)

An archeologist restores a large ceramic vessel of American Indian origin and typical of the type used for storage. (Photo: VDHR)

This de Bry engraving, based on a John White watercolor, shows a ceramic vessel being heated in a fire. (From the collections of The Mariners' Museum, Newport News, Va.)

Pamunkey Indians still make pottery using a centuries-old technique to shape clay dug from the banks of the Pamunkey River. Visitors to the Pamunkey Indian Reservation, located adjacent to King William County, Virginia, can purchase pottery in the Pamunkey Indian Museum and Gift Shop. This photograph shows the late Dora Cook Bradby making pottery in the Pamunkey Pottery School in the 1980s. The Mattaponi Indian Reservation is also located adjacent to King William County, along the banks of the Mattaponi River. Both reservations are among the nation's oldest, pre-dating the formation of the United States, established when Virginia was an English colony. (Photo: Pamunkey Museum)

85

worked as field technicians. Lynn Ripley joined the crew on a daily basis. Bob Ripley helped move people and equipment across the property and documented the work through photographs. Work at Werowocomoco continued every summer from 2003 through 2007, and again in 2009 and 2010. During that time, the research group invited elected officials to tour the site, hosted teachers and students from Gloucester County, and helped organize an "open house" week for Virginia Indians. Lynn Ripley's workshop became a professional archeological laboratory. Students in the William and Mary field school slept in tents and swam in the river to cool off. But while all of this activity buzzed across the land, the real story unfolded from below. The green fields that wrapped around the Ripleys' house were systematically peeled back to reveal squares of packed brown earth, where the remnants of Werowocomoco lay waiting. Excavations revealed an age and depth to the site that no one in the research group had expected to find.

The first surprise came from the shoreline. Brown and Harpole's survey recovered the greatest density of artifacts and features from the bluff above Purtan Bay, about 300 feet from the Ripleys' house. The fieldwork continued to recover a dense assortment of pottery pieces, projectile points, and stone flakes. Postmold stains, typically left by the saplings that were cut and erected to support the walls of Indian houses, were scattered across the site. The area clearly hosted a series of residential occupations, but the overlapping construction of houses and uneven preservation of post stains make it difficult to isolate the footprint of individual dwellings.

This portion of shoreline appears to have been the residential core of Werowocomoco, including areas of land that eroded away and are now underwater. But the human presence at Purtan Bay dates back much earlier than Powhatan's residence. Archeological evidence now suggests that a sizable town was established there as early as the year 1200—and people had visited periodically for thousands of years prior. A fragment of a bean, about three-eighths of an inch long, was a very special find: radiocarbon analysis returned the earliest date on record for cultivated beans in the Virginia Coastal Plain, suggesting that raising beans became a farming practice here at least as early as the 1400s.

Volunteers and archeologists work on excavation blocks situated near the bluff along Purtan Bay. Here a dense assortment of pottery pieces, projectile points, and stone flakes were recovered. Postmold stains were also scattered across the site. (Photos: WRG)

Corn

The botanical remains of corn are an important mark in the archeological record. Archeologists believe that when Indians of the Chesapeake region began planting corn and squash about 600 years ago, they also began creating towns. They still hunted game, fished the water, and gathered plants from the woods, but their social life and yearly cycle were centered on the planting and harvesting of corn. "Corn is central to understanding the Virginia Algonquian world," said archeologist Martin Gallivan. "Their sense of time and place was tied to where the corn was grown, and riverside towns like Werowocomoco anchored their lives."

Several fragments of corn, two of which date to the 1300s, were also found along the shoreline.

Another shoreline excavation took place about 300 feet inland, closer to the Ripleys' house. Here, archeologists found evidence dating as far back as 100 BCE, including the remains of plants, fragments of ceramics, native post-mold stains, and stone artifacts of quartz, quartzite, and jasper. There were also several concentrations of oyster shells. These deposits accumulated in a residential area containing dense and overlapping postmold patterns that occurred over generations. Taken together, the evidence suggests repeated seasonal settlements associated with oyster harvesting and processing along the riverside bluff between 100 BCE and 1300 CE.

Archeologists also explored a large field set back from the water, between the Ripleys' house and the tree line. Results from the central area of this field were striking because so few artifacts or native features were found there. "Excavations closer to the riverfront turned up dense deposits of artifacts and postmold patterns, but we only found a few artifacts in this central area and no intact features or postmolds," said Gallivan.

While this might suggest that researchers had found the boundary of Werowocomoco's active acreage, the earlier survey by Brown and Harpole showed that Indian features and artifacts extended well beyond this point. The gap in artifacts, as it turns out, was no accident. The landscape at Werowocomoco appears to have been organized into separate areas. Based on the evidence recovered to date, the research group believes that daily, secular life took place along the water, distinct from a large, inner sanctum that lay farther inland—an area marked by spiritual and political power. It was also marked, literally, by a special feature in the land that had been sketched on the Zuñiga map in 1608.

Volunteers and students work pasture excavation pits during the 2005 summer field school. (Photos: WRG)

Postmold

When archeologists speak of a postmold, they are referring to a feature below the plowzone that shows the evidence in the ground of a post after the wood has rotted away. It is typically identified by the darker color of the soil. This photograph clearly shows postmolds outlining the oval shape of a American Indian house that archeologists excavated in a modern neighborhood in the eastern Tidewater area of Virginia. (Photo: VDHR)

Chapter 8
Double Trenches and the Space Within

The Zuñiga map is one of two maps from 1608 that depict the location of Werowocomoco. On it, two sites marking human occupation stand out above the rest. One is James Fort. The mapmaker drew the fort as a triangle with flared and rounded corners, reflecting the shape the fort would take if viewed from above. This is an accurate depiction of the fort's structure, as described in the historical record and confirmed by archeologists who have studied the fort's remains.

At Werowocomoco, the Zuñiga map includes a symbol that has been described as a "double D." The flat edge of the D-shape faces the water, while the arc of the D curves inland. Its lines are doubled, similar to an image that has been blurred, or possibly a thick letter D that has been outlined in black on both sides with a white interior. Historians and archeologists assumed this marked a large Indian town, as would be expected for Powhatan's headquarters. The exact meaning of the shape, or the three dots inside it, was unknown.

This detail from the Zuñiga Chart (see Chapter 5) clearly shows a symbol for Werowocomoco. Its appearance has been described as a "double D." Here, the flat edge of the D-shape faces the present day York River, while the arc of the D curves inland.

In 2003, archeologists began to find answers. A portion of two trenches was uncovered in the field behind the Ripleys' house, about a thousand feet from Purtan Bay. The trenches were indicated by a band of dark soil between 3- and 5-feet wide and between 1- to 3-feet deep; over time, this darker soil had filled the void of the trenches. The trenches themselves cut across the field in parallel lines about 4 and 7 feet apart. At first, researchers thought the trenches might have been dug for an early colonial farm. After all, the field had been farmed for centuries; archeologists had located artifacts from an early homestead nearby; and the use of ditches to drain farm fields and mark property was common practice. But over the next few years, the research team made some surprising discoveries.

During the 2003 field school, archeological investigations revealed Werowocomoco's trench features, clearly seen in this photograph as two parallel bands of darker colored soil, a result of organically-rich topsoil washing back into the trenches over the centuries to gradually fill them. (Photo: WRG)

A close-up profile of the same trench feature shown in the photograph above of the trench excavation. The lighter-hued soil is the sub soil, representing the base of the trench feature. (Photo: WRG)

First, the trenches mark a very long line. On the north side, their path is lost in the woods. In the other direction, where the trenches run through open field, the path measures 690 feet—more than twice the length of a football field. "I thought they might go on for a hundred feet or so," said archeologist Martin Gallivan. "But they go much, much farther. We quickly realized that this is something special."

Evidence also indicates that Indians, not colonists, dug the trenches. The research team found only a few English artifacts from the 1600s near the top of the trenches and no farm-related artifacts from later periods in the soil that filled them. Instead, they found native ceramics, evidence of stone tools, and plant remains. Digging the trenches would have removed a large amount of soil that could have been used for erecting earthworks, but no trace of such structures has been detected. There is also no evidence of postholes in the trenches, which would have indicated its use as a wall or barrier. At the bottom of the trenches, which potentially represents the time at which they were created, researchers found remnants of wood charcoal and corn. The radiocarbon dates from some of these materials suggest that the trenches were dug and filled in over a period of several hundred years, from the 1200s through approximately 1560.

Radiocarbon Dating

Radiocarbon dating helps archeologists determine the age of organic objects, such as wood, bone, or shell. All living things absorb radiocarbon from the air or their diet. When an organism dies, the amount of radiocarbon in its remains begins to decrease at a very steady rate. The amount of radiocarbon that exists in an artifact gives researchers a very accurate sense of when it lived. At Werowocomoco, radiocarbon dating identified the age of corn, bits of beans, and charred wood in the trenches—all of which reveals information about the years in which people were using them.

On the longest excavated path, the trenches run almost due north and south across the field. At the end point that was excavated in the field, they make a sharp turn inland, to the east, and begin to curve. The full path has not been excavated, but it roughly matches the shape of the double D on Zuñiga's map, thought to be a copy of John Smith's field renderings. "When I started to realize that the D-shape matched what we were seeing on the ground, I was blown away," Gallivan said. "It's incredible to think that Smith—or whoever created the Zuñiga map—may have drawn something that we actually found in the archeological record."

Indians used earthworks to define monumental places in other parts of eastern North America. But until the excavation of these features at Werowocomoco, no monumental-scale architecture had been identified in the Chesapeake region. Of the few trenches identified in the region, none approach the scale of those at Werowocomoco.

The presence and size of the trenches suggest that Werowocomoco was an extremely important place. But their age suggests something more. The paired trenches at Werowocomoco date to the period between 1350 and the early 1600s, and a smaller trench just east of these features was constructed in the 1200s—up to 400 years before Powhatan's chiefdom. This means that Werowocomoco was an important place well before Powhatan lived there. Werowocomoco did not become powerful because of Powhatan; the power was there before him. Powhatan chose to enhance his political and spiritual influence by living at a place that had carried great meaning for centuries.

No one yet knows why Werowocomoco acquired this importance but, to the archeologists, the area marked by trenches is a critical part of the landscape. There are no postmold stains inside the trenches. Although soil may have been mounded up between the trenches, they appear to have been a visual boundary and not the base of a fortified wall. A small break in the trenches marks an entrance to the area that appears to have been enclosed by the trenches. Archeologists have discovered artifacts and several features inside this space that have yet to be explained. The smaller single trench, which predates the double trenches, runs parallel to the larger set. It has strongly defined corners, but the rest of its shape disappears in an area heavily disturbed by plows.

Still farther inland, almost at the tree line, the research team made another important find—postmolds from the largest Indian house pattern yet discovered in the Chesapeake region. The researchers believe it could be a house used by Powhatan himself. The house is located inside the trenched area, which archeologists interpret as a place of importance, kept separate from ordinary houses. It was also unusually large. English colonists of the early 1600s noted that houses of chiefs were bigger than the homes of ordinary Indians. Archeologists working in Virginia have found that typical longhouses measured about 15- to 30-feet long and 10- to 18-feet wide. The structure inside the trenches is more than twice this size, stretching 72 feet in length and 20 feet in width. Of the longhouses identified to date at Werowocomoco, only the structure inside the trenches comes close to Smith's estimated length of 80 to 100 feet. Many postmold stains overlap in this area, some of which form lines that suggest partition walls inside the structure. This is similar to a description by Henry Spelman in his *1609 Relation of Virginia*, which noted, "The king's houses are both broader and longer then the rest having many dark windings and turnings before any come where the king is."

Smith also mentions that Powhatan's house was a considerable distance from the water, so far that he was uncomfortable when Captain Christopher Newport agreed to meet with Powhatan while sending his guards back to the boat. Smith describes the distance as "thirty score." A score is a set of 20, so 30 score equals 600. But it's not clear whether Smith meant 600 feet, 600 paces (roughly 1,500 feet) or 600 yards (1,800 feet). Measured in a straight line, however, the large longhouse is about 1,300 feet from Purtan Bay. Shoreline has been lost to erosion, so the distance to the waterfront would have been longer when Smith walked it. The research team concluded that, if Smith were measuring in paces, the distance between the recovered longhouse and the waterfront matches Smith's description fairly well.

Copper pieces have also been found near the longhouse—copper that suggests a direct link to the colonists at James Fort. Lynn Ripley had collected about 20 pieces near the site of the longhouse before the systematic fieldwork began. Eleven more pieces were found during excavations. Most were in small sheets, relatively flat with dents and rough edges, about an inch square. Some had been rolled into long cylinders that could be worn as beads, and a few were shaped into flat, round discs. The area appears to have been a concentrated location for copper artifacts; to date, only one piece has been found elsewhere on the property.

According to the archeologists, two things make the location of this copper special. First, copper was the mark of a leader. Copper was rare among Virginia Algonquians and was highly valued, with both ritual and spiritual significance. A leader who held much copper had access to influence or power. Second, scientists compared the copper pieces with similar pieces recovered at James Fort. The colonists had brought scrap copper with them from England and used it in trade with the Indians, especially for corn. Results of the analysis showed that the chemical footprints of the copper pieces are nearly identical. This strongly suggests that the copper at Werowocomoco probably came from James Fort. Based on the presence of copper, along with the location, size, and age of the longhouse, the Werowocomoco Research Group believes that this structure was indeed associated with Powhatan—and may have been the same place that Smith described in his written accounts.

After the field sessions drew to a close in 2010, archeologist Randolph Turner made another unexpected observation. At dawn on the summer solstice, the sun at Werowocomoco rises above the tree line at the rear of the field where the trenches and the longhouse were found. As the sun peeks above the trees, it falls into a direct line with what may have been Powhatan's longhouse and with an entrance through the trenches. There is no way to know if this alignment was intentional. Evidence from historical accounts of the Chesapeake region, however, suggests that east was a sacred direction. Virginia Algonquian "temples" in other locations had openings that faced east, and sacred fires were said to have been located in the eastern part of the temples. The research team speculated that Powhatan may have decided to place himself within an eastern alignment, both to demonstrate his power and to extend it.

Opposite: Sunrise on summer solstice at Werowocomoco in a photo taken by property owner Bob Ripley. It's an intriguing image, evoking the site of Werowocomoco as a place of power, revealed by the sun's position. The two orange flags in the foreground mark a main passageway through the two trenches that archeologists theorize separated the secular and sacred areas of the site. Beyond the passage, the outline of a longhouse site that may have been associated with Powhatan (as revealed by postmolds archeologists uncovered) is depicted by the flags in the background, before the woods. The sun is directly aligned above both the passageway and the longhouse. (Photo: Bob Ripley)

The excavations that took place at Werowocomoco between 2003 and 2010 have confirmed the land's deep history. They have also raised many questions. Why did Werowocomoco evolve into a special, powerful place? What is the full path of the twin trenches? What structures lay on the inside of the trenches and how were they used? Clearly, Werowocomoco holds much potential for future research and, so far, only a small fraction of the site's total area has been studied. "This work is not even the tip of the iceberg," Turner said. "It's the tip of the tip."

Copper

Copper was highly valued in the Virginia Algonquian world. It was obtained from sources hundreds of miles away, most likely in what is now the Great Lakes region or Appalachian Mountains. Martin Gallivan of the College of William and Mary says that a full understanding of its value is complicated. "Material value is only one part of the story," Gallivan said. "Copper may have had spiritual value, too." Copper has a reddish hue, especially when hot or shiny. Red is one of three colors—red, black, and white—that played an important part in ceremonial activities. "In the Powhatan world, copper was worn by werowances [chiefs or leaders]; black was associated with priests; and white seemed to be associated with life," Gallivan said.

Trade copper recovered from the Werowocomoco site. Chemical analysis indicates that these artifacts originated from Jamestown's copper supply. (Photo: WRG)

Chapter 9
Virginia Indians Today

Indians associated with the Powhatan era did not disappear with Werowocomoco or in the centuries that followed. Today, the ancestors of eight of the tribes associated with the Powhatan chiefdom have persisted and honored their heritage while enduring violence and racism and losing most of their traditional lands. These tribes include the Chickahominy, Eastern Chickahominy, Nansemond, Mattaponi, Upper Mattaponi, Pamunkey, Patawomeck, and Rappahannock. Seven of the tribes have pursued official recognition from the federal government.

Contemporary Virginia Tribes Associated with Powhatan

The Chickahominy
(Based in Charles City County; 110 acres; 840 tribal members)

Website: www.chickahominytribe.org

The Chickahominy live near the Chickahominy River, a few miles from the area their ancestors occupied when Jamestown was founded. Chickahominy villages lined the river, starting about 15 miles from its mouth near Jamestown to the middle of what is now New Kent County.

Because the Chickahominy lived so close to the Jamestown settlement, they had early contact with the colonists. They traded food for English items during the first few winters, which helped the English survive, and later taught them how to grow and preserve their own food. Captain John Smith made several trading expeditions up the Chickahominy River.

English expansion forced the Chickahominy from their homeland. The treaty of 1646 granted the tribe land in the Pamunkey Neck area of Virginia, near the present day Mattaponi reservation. The tribe lost their reservation over time and began migrating to Chickahominy Ridge, where most of its members now live. They bought land for homes and established the Samaria Baptist Church,

The Mattaponi and Pamunkey Reservations

The Mattaponi and Pamunkey are the only two tribes in Virginia to own reservations. Both are located adjacent to King William County, about 20 miles east of Richmond. The Mattaponi reservation covers approximately 150 acres along the Mattaponi River, and the Pamunkey reservation covers approximately 1,200 acres along the Pamunkey River.

The Mattaponi and Pamunkey reservations are among the oldest in the United States. Both date back to treaties signed with the English in 1646 and 1677 respectively, and their land base was established as early as 1658. The Mattaponi and Pamunkey have continuously honored the terms of the treaties, which require a yearly tribute of fish and game. Every November, on the Wednesday before Thanksgiving, tribal members travel to Richmond and present the governor with a gift of deer or turkey.

While the Mattaponi and Pamunkey are the only reservations in Virginia today, there were independent Indian towns at various times in the history of the state, including the towns of Chickahominy and Rappahannock.

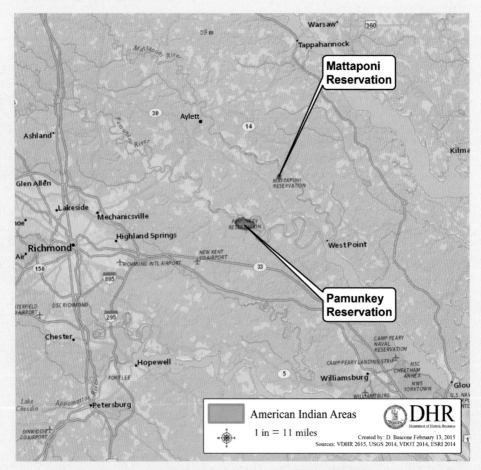

The Pamunkey and Mattaponi Reservations are located on the Pamunkey and Mattaponi Rivers, which come together at West Point to form the York River. (VDHR)

which serves as an important community focal point. Years later, they also purchased land for tribal use and built a tribal center. The Chickahominy Fall Festival and Powwow takes place there every year in September.

When the English first arrived, the Chickahominy were led by a council of elders and religious leaders called mungai or "great men." Today, the tribe is led by a tribal council elected by the votes of tribal members. The council is made up of 12 men and women, including a chief and two assistant chiefs. Most of the Chickahominy live within a 5-mile radius of the tribal center, but several hundred more live in other parts of the country. The Chickahominy Tribe is recognized by the Commonwealth of Virginia and, since 1996, has been working to become officially recognized by the United States.

The Eastern Chickahominy

(Based in New Kent County; 41 acres; 164 tribal members)

Website: www.cied.org

The Eastern Chickahominy, officially known as the Chickahominy Indians Eastern Division, shared a history with the Chickahominy Tribe until the early 20th century, when they decided to form their own tribal government. The Eastern Chickahominy government was formally organized in 1920–21, with Edward P. Bradby as chief, and a certificate of incorporation was issued to the tribe in 1925. A one-room schoolhouse opened for the Eastern Chickahominy in 1910, which served grades one through eight. It was also the meeting place for the Tsena Commocko Indian Baptist Church, organized in

September 1922, until construction of their church was complete. Today, the Eastern Chickahominy have built a tribal center and museum in which to hold functions in fellowship with out-of-state-visitors and enrich the lives of tribal and non-tribal members alike.

Most of the Eastern Chickahominy live in Virginia, but approximately 80 members live out of state. Tribal members work in such areas as technology, nursing, business administration, and privately owned businesses. At least 26 of its members have served in the U.S. Armed Forces since World War I. The Eastern Chickahominy has been seeking federal recognition since the 1990s.

Federal Recognition

Six Virginia tribes are seeking federal recognition through an act of Congress since the late 1990s: the Upper Mattaponi, the Chickahominy, the Eastern Chickahominy, the Nansemond, the Rappahannock, and the Monacan Nation. Meanwhile, the Pamunkey tribe is seeking federal recognition through the Bureau of Indian Affairs.

Federal recognition brings respect and the right to self-government, and includes eligibility for scholarships and federal funds for housing, health care, and economic development. Federal recognition also protects tribal heritage through the American Indian Graves Protection and Repatriation Act, which allows the tribes to petition for the return of ancestral bones and funeral objects to be reburied with respect.

Federal recognition can be granted through the Bureau of Indian Affairs or by an act of Congress. Tribes that petition for federal recognition through the Bureau of Indian Affairs must document their existence as a sustained community since historical times. However, past policies in Virginia have made this a difficult task. Walter Ashby Plecker, head of Vital Statistics in Virginia from 1912–1946, with the support of the Racial Integrity Act enacted by the Virginia General Assembly in 1924, worked to remove Indian identities from the written record, replacing the term "Indian" with "colored" on many birth and death certificates, marriage licenses, and voter registration forms. The organization and activism of Indians in the early 20th century was in part an act of resistance to the policy of "paper genocide" that was in place at the time. The Racial Integrity Act was deemed unconstitutional in 1967 by a decision of the U.S. Supreme Court, in Loving v. Virginia, which effectively ended Virginia's ban on interracial marriage. Later, the act was repealed by the General Assembly in 1975 but the act and Plecker's administrative work had profoundly disrupted the documentation of Indian heritage in Virginia.

Federal recognition for Virginia Indians has also been complicated by the requirement that nation-to-nation treaty negotiations have occurred between the tribes and the United States government. Indians in Virginia signed treaties in the 1600s, long before the United States was formed.

The Mattaponi

(Based along the Mattaponi River, King William County; 150 acres; 450 tribal members)
Website: none to date.

The Mattaponi Indian Reservation along the Mattaponi River. (Photo: Mark Custalow)

The Mattaponi have one of the oldest reservations in the United States and are one of only two tribes in Virginia, along with the Pamunkey, that own reservation lands. Approximately 75 tribal members live on the reservation, which includes living quarters, a church, a museum, pottery shops, and a community building that was once the reservation school. The reservation is also home to the tribe's Hatchery and Marine Science Facility, which supports the tribe's traditional shad fishery and promotes the restoration of the shad population and stewardship of the river. Their programs include fish tagging, water quality monitoring, and the development of educational materials about protecting water resources.

The Mattaponi have their own sovereign government made up of the chief, assistant chief, and seven councilmen. They aim to maintain a sustainable community that will continue the thousands of years of Mattaponi history and heritage and, in so doing, demonstrate how everyone can live successful and rewarding lives in harmony with the earth.

The Upper Mattaponi

(Based in King William County; 32 acres; 575 tribal members)
Website: www.uppermattaponi.org

When the English arrived in 1607, the ancestors of the Upper Mattaponi were among the prosperous communities associated with Powhatan's chiefdom. Captain John Smith's 1612 map shows a village called Passaunkack in the same area where the tribe is currently located.

Feather weaving was a tradition among tribes. This turkey feather cape was woven in the 1930s by Mollie Adams, wife of Upper Mattaponi Chief Jasper Adams. (Jamestown-Yorktown Foundation collection)

In the mid-1600s, other tribes had been forced by the English into the upper reaches of the Mattaponi River. A map by Augustine Herman see (pg. 6) in 1673 shows the largest concentration of Indians near Passaunkack. The Pamunkey leader, Cockacoeske, signed the Treaty of 1677 on behalf of the Upper Mattaponi, and a reservation was established near Passaunkack for both the

Chickahominy and Mattaponi. The Chickahominy moved back to their homeland in the 1700s; those that remained are the ancestors of the Upper Mattaponi.

Through the 1700s and 1800s, the Upper Mattaponi were called the Adamstown band because so many tribal members had the last name of Adams. A core group of at least 10 Adamstown families were documented there by 1850. An 1863 Civil War map showed the area as Indian Land, and by the 1880s the Adamstown Band had its own school. Although the racial climate limited Indian rights and made it difficult for Indians to prosper, the tribe valued education; in 1892 the first federal funds were requested for education of the Adamstown Indians.

In the early 1900s, the tribe officially took on the name of Upper Mattaponi. The Sharon Indian School, a one-room schoolhouse, was built in 1919 and used until 1952, when a brick structure was built next to the original school. After desegregation in 1965, the school was closed. It is now on the Virginia Landmarks Register and the National Register of Historic Places and is still used for tribal meetings and cultural gatherings.

Most of the Upper Mattaponi converted to Christianity by the 1800s and worshipped in their homes or other Indian churches, in particular the churches on the Pamunkey and Mattaponi reservations. In the early 1900s, church services were held in the Sharon Indian School until the tribe built a new church, the Indian View Baptist Church, in 1942. Homecoming is held on the grounds every summer and hundreds of Upper Mattaponi, as well as dozens of Indians from other Virginia tribes, gather there. The tribe also purchased land where they hold cultural events, and they plan to develop a new tribal center.

Members of the Upper Mattaponi have maintained their tribal identity while also becoming physicians, pharmacists, accountants, and business owners. The tribe has been working for federal recognition since the 1990s.

Chief Barry Bass, Nansemond Indian Tribe, and his wife, Betty.

The Nansemond

(Based in Suffolk and Chesapeake; 200 tribal members)
Website: www.nansemond.org

When the English first arrived, the Nansemond lived in villages along the Nansemond River centered near Chuckatuck (present-day Suffolk). The chief, as well as the tribe's temples and sacred items, were on Dumpling Island. The tribe numbered about 1,200 people, with 300 bowmen.

In 1608, the English raided the Nansemond towns, burning houses and destroying canoes, to force the Indians to give up their corn. The raids began open hostilities between the two peoples. The tribe had to relocate on several occasions as Europeans continued to move into the Nansemond River basin. The Nansemond lost their last known reservation lands by 1792.

Today, most Nansemond live in or near the cities of Suffolk, Chesapeake, Norfolk, Virginia Beach, and Portsmouth. Monthly meetings are held at the Indiana United Methodist Church, which was founded in 1850 as a mission for the tribe and is adjacent to the site of earlier tribal schools. Tribal members operate a museum and gift shop in Chuckatuck (Suffolk). The tribe also hopes to build a tribal center, museum, and living history area at the site of Mattanock, an ancient town of their ancestors. The tribe has received 68 riverfront acres from the city of Suffolk, where they would like to reconstruct Mattanock in order to provide a center for their tribe and draw visitors to the site.

The Nansemond co-host a powwow every June and hold their annual powwow each August. The tribe has been seeking federal recognition since the 1990s.

The Pamunkey
(Based along the Pamunkey River, King William County; 1,200 acres; 200 tribal members)
Website: www.pamunkey.net

The Pamunkey referred to themselves as the most powerful tribe in the Powhatan chiefdom, because of their dense population, ready supply of warriors, and pivotal leadership. The modern Pamunkey are proud of their history and the bravery their ancestors showed against the encroaching Englishmen. Today, the Pamunkey are one of only two tribes in Virginia, along with the Mattaponi, that own reservation lands. The 1677 Treaty of Middle Plantation, which helped to establish the reservations, was signed by the female Pamunkey leader, Cockacoeske, on behalf of several Virginia Indian tribes.

Native use of the Pamunkey reservation land dates back 10 to 12 thousand years. In 1979, the Pamunkey built a museum on the reservation to portray the history and culture of their people. Today, approximately 50 tribal members live on the reservation itself; others live in Richmond, Newport News, other parts of Virginia, and across the United States.

Pamunkey Indian J. Henry Langston milking eggs from a female shad on the Pamunkey River in 2001. The Pamunkey and Mattaponi tribes still operate shad hatcheries at their respective reservations. (Photo: The Mariners' Museum, Newport News, Va.)

The Pamunkey governing body consists of a chief and seven council members that are elected every four years. Elections are held in the traditional manner, with a corn kernel used for a "yes" vote and a pea for a "no" vote. The person with the most corn is elected. The governing body is responsible for all tribal governmental functions as set forth by their laws. The tribe administers all of the laws itself.

The Pamunkey no longer rely exclusively on making pottery, fishing, hunting, and trapping to make a living, but they have preserved close ties to these traditions. The Pamunkey still make pottery in the traditional manner and have done so continuously since aboriginal times. The tribe is also proud that its members have served in the U.S. Armed Forces during every war and major conflict since the American Revolution.

Chief John Lightner, Patawomeck Tribe. (Photo: John Lightner)

The Patawomeck
(Based in Stafford County; 1,500 tribal members)
Website: www.patawomeckindiantribeofvirginia.org

The Patawomeck first encountered the English when Captain John Smith visited the tribe in 1608. At times, they befriended the English and provided food. The Patawomeck were part of the Powhatan Federation of Tribes when Captain Smith visited the tribe in 1608, according to writings of Henry Spelman, who lived with the tribe. They appear to have severed that relationship about 1622 when they refused to give Chief Opechancanough support in killing the English.

In 1609, Francis West was sent from James Fort to get corn from the Patawomeck, but instead beheaded two of them and sailed back to England. Captain Samuel Argall later traded with the Patawomeck for much food during the "Starving Time" at the fort. According to an English source, Pocahontas was with the tribe in 1613. When Argall learned of this, he kidnapped her in order to force her father Powhatan to return English prisoners and stolen weapons.

In the 1650s, settlers began moving into Patawomeck territory. Pressures and violence followed. The Patawomeck sold their remaining land to the colonists in 1665. After war was declared by the English in 1666, the Patawomeck disappear from the historical record. In 1928, an anthropologist named Frank Speck wrote about Virginia Indians living around the original Patawomeck capital. He believed these to be descendants of the Patawomeck, although he called them "Potomac" as he did not have solid proof for his theory.

The Patawomeck Tribal Historian William L. Deyo conducted years of research and prepared documentation in 1996 to show that the current tribe was descended from the Patawomeck tribe of the 1600s. Many members of the current tribe worked together over the following years to preserve the heritage of the tribe through customs, crafts, hunting, and fishing. In 2008 the tribe began, through the leadership of Becky Guy, to teach the Algonquian language of the ancestors, based on the vocabulary preserved from the writings of Captain John Smith and William Strachey, the colonial secretary of Virginia. As a result of those efforts, the Patawomeck were presented with a 2008 Historic Preservation Award for their "earnest efforts to revive their native language and preserve their culture for future generations of native peoples in Stafford County." In 2010, the Patawomeck sought state recognition through the Virginia General Assembly. Entertainer, Wayne Newton, a Patawomeck Tribal member, cancelled a show in Las Vegas to testify in front of the Virginia House and Senate in support of their bid for state recognition. House Joint Resolution No. 150, which cited the documentation amassed by William Deyo, was unanimously approved by both the House of Delegates and the Senate. On February 18, 2010, the Patawomeck Tribe was officially granted state recognition.

July 2006. Members of the Rappahannock Tribe pose with their English host during an event at Cobham Hall, built in 1594, in Gravesend, Kent, England. Tribal members were part of an official delegation of Virginia Indians that visited England. (Photo: VDHR)

Rappahannock Tribe

(Based in Indian Neck, King and Queen County;
132 acres; 300 tribal members)
Website: www.rappahannocktribe.org

The Rappahannock encountered Englishmen in 1603, before the founding of Jamestown, when a small English crew was exploring the Rappahannock River. The Rappahannock chief befriended the captain, but the captain then killed the chief and kidnapped a group of Rappahannock men, who were taken to England. Later that year, these men were reportedly demonstrating the use of dugout canoes on the Thames River in London.

The Rappahannock met Captain John Smith in December 1607, at their capital of Topahanocke. Opechancanough had captured Smith and brought him to the town so the people could determine if Smith was the same man who had murdered their chief and kidnapped their men in 1603. Smith was not the same man. In 1608, he returned to the area and mapped 14 Rappahannock towns on the north side of the river. The south side of the river was primarily the tribe's hunting grounds.

In the 1640s, the English began settling the Rappahannock River valley. Following Bacon's Rebellion in 1676, the Rappahannock moved into one village. In November of 1682, the Rappahannock were given a 3,474-acre reservation in Indian Neck. The following year, the Virginia Colony forcibly removed the tribe, relocating them to the frontier to act as human shields between white Virginians and the New York Iroquois, who were attacking the settlers. Rappahannock descendants eventually returned to the Virginia land. Many live there today, although the land itself is no longer a reservation.

The Rappahannock incorporated in 1921, in an effort to solidify their tribal government and gain state recognition. By 1997, two phases of construction were complete on their cultural center, and in 1998 they elected the first female chief since 1705, G. Anne Richardson. Chief Richardson is a fourth-generation chief in her family, with a legacy of traditional leadership and service. Also in 1998, the tribe purchased 110 acres and established a land trust for building a housing development. The first home was sold in 2001.

Every year, the Rappahannock host their Harvest Festival and Pow-wow on the second Saturday in October at their Cultural Center in Indian Neck. They also have a drum group, called the Maskapow ("Little Beaver"), and a traditional dance group called the Rappahannock American Indian Dancers. The groups perform both locally and abroad to share the tribe's history and traditions. In 1996, the Rappahannock again began seeking federal recognition, building on Chief George Nelson's 1921 petition to the U.S. Congress for recognition of the tribe's civil and sovereign rights.

Other Contemporary Tribes in Virginia

In addition to the Algonquian tribes listed above, Virginia has tribes of Siouan (the Monacan) and Iroquoian (the Nottoway and Cheroenhaka) affiliation.

Chapter 10
Places to Visit

The Virginia Indian Heritage Trail

http://virginiahumanities.org/virginia-indian-program/

The Virginia Indian Heritage Trail is a collection of tribal sites and interpretive sites where you can learn more about Virginia Indians past and present. Information about the trail is contained in a book, *The Virginia Heritage Trail*, now only available as a PDF. The downloadable publication is available online at the web address above, under "resources." The trail includes sites of some tribes whose ancestors were associated with the Powhatan chiefdom:

Mattaponi Indian Reservation

Museum, shad fish hatchery, pottery shop, and trading post

1413 Mattaponi Reservation Circle
West Point, VA 23181

Saturdays and Sundays 10 a.m.-4 p.m. or by appointment.

Contact: George Custalow (804) 769-2229

Pamunkey Indian Reservation

Museum, shad fish hatchery, pottery school, Tribal Council complex, and Pamunkey Baptist Church

Pamunkey Indian Museum and Cultural Center
175 Lay Landing Rd.
King William, VA 23086
Contact: (804) 843-4792

Rappahannock Tribal Center

5036 Indian Neck Road
Indian Neck, VA 23148

Open by appointment

Contact: Chief Richardson
info@rappahannocktribe.org

Along the Captain John Smith Chesapeake National Historic Trail (Photo: NPS © Middleton Evans)

The Captain John Smith Chesapeake National Historic Trail

www.smithtrail.net and www.nps.gov/cajo

The Captain John Smith Chesapeake National Historic Trail follows the routes of Smith's travels based on his map and journals. It encompasses Smith's two main voyages on the Chesapeake Bay in 1608 and also his excursions on the York, James, and other rivers between 1607 and 1609. The trail, administered by the National Park Service, covers approximately 3,000 miles in parts of Virginia, Maryland, Delaware, the District of Columbia, New York and Pennsylvania. The trail offers many boating opportunities and land-based sites for learning about the 17th-century landscape and the American Indians Smith encountered on his travels.

The Captain John Smith Geotrail is a family-friendly geocaching adventure. Geocaching is an outdoor game using GPS coordinates to find a hidden container with token treasures inside. Geocache rules allow you to keep one token and leave one behind for others to find. The Captain John Smith Geotrail includes more than 50 hidden caches on seven rivers that represent scenes from Smith's adventures around the Chesapeake Bay. For more information, visit www.smithtrail.net. For the basics of geocaching, visit www.geocaching.com.

To explore the trail by water, browse the routes on the Smith Trail website or follow the official *Boater's Guide to the Captain John Smith Chesapeake National Historic Trail*. The Boater's Guide weaves together history, geography, and practical information for seeing the Chesapeake Bay by water, for all types of vessels and skill levels. The Boater's Guide can be viewed and downloaded in whole or by river segment from www.smithtrail.net.

Youth ages 6 through 12 can earn a Junior Ranger Badge for the John Smith Trail from the National Park Service. To earn the badge, participating youth complete a series of workbook activities that help them learn about Smith's voyages, the Chesapeake Bay, and American Indians. For information about the program or to download the activity book, click on "For Kids" at www.nps.gov/cajo or visit www.smithtrail.net.

The only 17th-century building remaining in Jamestown is the tower of the James City Parish Church, owned by Preservation Virginia.

Historic Jamestowne

https://historicjamestowne.org and www.nps.gov/jame

Historic Jamestowne is the original site of James Fort and the first permanent English settlement in North America. In 1996, archeologists discovered the footprint of James Fort and the story of Jamestown is now being retold. But while the site itself marks the beginning of English colonial ventures, archeologists at Historic Jamestowne tell a broader story about the intersection of three diverse cultures—Indian, European, and African—and the society they made together. Visitors can watch the archeologists at work on site, take guided tours, enjoy special programs, walk the grounds at their own pace, and explore exhibits in the visitor center and museum. Exhibits include European and Indian artifacts found at the fort and townsite and explore the cultural exchange that took place during the early 1600s.

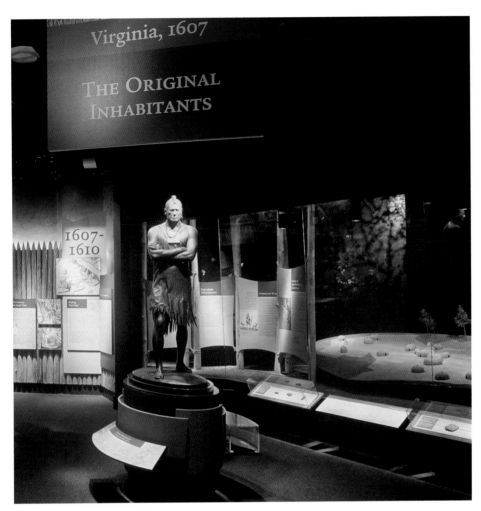

The galleries at Jamestown Settlement. (Photo: Jamestown-Yorktown Foundation)

Jamestown Settlement

http://www.historyisfun.org/jamestown-settlement/

Jamestown Settlement, a living-history museum of 17th-century Virginia, features expansive gallery exhibits and an introductory film that describe the cultures of the Powhatan Indians, Europeans, and Africans who converged in 1600s Virginia and trace Jamestown's beginnings in England and the first century of the Virginia Colony. Outdoors, historical interpreters depict daily life in a re-created 1610–14 fort, three 1607 ships and in a re-created Powhatan Indian village. The re-created Powhatan Indian village is based on archeological findings at a site once inhabited by the Paspahegh, the tribe in whose territory Jamestown was established, and on descriptions recorded by English colonists.

Visitors are invited to help with hands-on activities that demonstrate the ways in which Indians grew and prepared food, crafted canoes from felled trees, processed animal hides, made tools and pottery, and wove plant fibers into cordage.

Open 9 a.m. to 5 p.m. daily;
closed Christmas and New Year's days.
Call (757) 253-4838 or toll-free (888) 593-4682.

Henricus Historical Park

http://www.henricus.org/

Commemorating 400 years, Henricus Historical Park re-creates everyday 17th-century life in the second successful English settlement in North America and resides on the original site of the Citie of Henricus. Due to its prime location as a military outpost on a bluff overlooking the James River, the site also boasts rich Civil War history. Surrounded by the Dutch Gap Conservation Area, the living-history museum offers Pre–K–12 and adult education programs, including indoor and outdoor meeting and special event space available for rental. Henricus Historical Park is a nonprofit organization that operates in partnership with the Henricus Foundation and the counties of Chesterfield and Henrico. For more information about Henricus Historical Park visit www.henricus.org.

Glossary

Algonquian Words

Indian groups in Tidewater Virginia spoke Virginia Algonquian. Over time, as generations of Indians grappled with the loss of land and lifeways, Virginia Algonquian was replaced by English. The only representation of the language as it existed in the early 1600s is in the written records of a few Englishmen. Some contemporary tribes and scholars have worked to reconstruct Virginia Algonquian, but much knowledge has been lost.

As English colonists tried to record Algonquian words, they created spellings to match what they heard. This led to a variety of spellings in historical records, written at a time in which even the spelling of English words varied greatly. As a result, there is no way to know exactly how Algonquian words were pronounced or what spelling best reflects their original sound.

Algonquian: A subfamily of American Indian languages

Appamattuck: Indians described by colonist William Strachey as living along the lower Appomattox River in the early 1600s, who Strachey said paid tribute to Powhatan

Arrohateck: An Indian town once located on what is now the James River, depicted on John Smith's 1608 map of the Chesapeake region

Cattapeuk: Early spring

Chiskiack: (or Kiskiack) An Indian town once located on what is now the York River, downstream and on the opposite shore from Werowocomoco, depicted on John Smith's 1608 map of the Chesapeake region

Cohattayough: Mid-spring to mid-summer

Mamanatowick: A title applied to Powhatan. To date there are no records of this title's being used for any other Indian leader, indicating that it was likely a title of great status. Mamanatowick is similar to a Northern Algonquian word for "gods."

Matoaka: The personal name of Pocahontas, prior to her taking the name Rebecca

Nepinough: Late summer to mid-fall, when corn and other crops were harvested

Opechancanough: A man often described as Powhatan's brother or half-brother, but who may have been a cousin of the same maternal line. Opechancanough led the Pamunkey and Youghtanund and served as a war leader to Powhatan. Shortly after Powhatan's death, he inherited leadership as paramount chief, a position he held until his death at the hands of the English in 1646.

Orapax: An Indian town that was once located on the headwaters of the Chickahominy River. Powhatan relocated to Orapax after leaving Werowocomoco in 1609.

Pamaunke: An early spelling of Pamunkey

Paspahegh: Indians in whose territory the Englishmen established the settlement of Jamestown

Pocahontas: An Indian girl and daughter of Powhatan, who lived at Werowocomoco when the English arrived in 1607. She later married John Rolfe and traveled to England, where she died.

Popanow: Late winter and early spring

Powhatan: An influential political and spiritual leader, who lived at Werowocomoco when the English arrived in 1607

Taquitock: Late fall and early winter

Tsenacomoco: A word thought to mean "densely populated place," used by modern writers to refer to the area now called the Virginia Tidewater. It is unclear as to exactly what geographical area it meant when it was used by Virginia Algonquians to the early English.

Utassantassa: (or tassantassee) A word used to describe the colonists, thought to mean "strangers"

Wahunsenacawh: The personal name of Powhatan

Werowance: A male chief or leader of an Indian community; a male, hereditary leader of a district or hamlet community

Weroansqua: A female leader of an Indian community

Werowocomoco: A long-standing Indian community that was the principal residence of Powhatan when the English arrived in 1607

Yihakan: (or ya'hacan) An Indian house

Youghtanund: Indians living along what is now the Pamunkey River when the English arrived in 1607

Other Terms to Know

Archeologist: A specialist in archeology; the scientific study of prehistoric and historic peoples and their cultures by analysis of their artifacts, inscriptions, monuments, etc.

Archeological Survey: A type of field research by which archeologists search for archeological sites and collect information about the location, distribution, and organization of past human cultures across a large area

Artifact: An object or the remains of one made by humans that represents and reflects a specific culture and cultural time

Chastened: When used in reference to the land this means to subdue or restrain in ability

Chief: A leader of a group of people; an individual that holds the highest authority

Chiefdom: The area and scope to which a chief rules

Commemoration: A ceremony focused on remembering a person and/or event

Confluence: To come together

Continental Shelf: A continental shelf is the edge of a continent that lies under the ocean. Continents are the seven main divisions of land on Earth. A continental shelf extends from the coastline of a continent to a drop-off point called the shelf break. (National Geographic Society)

Coronation: A ceremony that crowns a new leader, such as a king or queen

Cultural Anthropologist: The branch of anthropology dealing with the origins, history, and development of human culture, and including in its scope the fields of archeology, ethnology, and ethnography

Cultural Landscape: A geographic area, including both cultural and natural resources and the wildlife or domestic animals therein, associated with a historic event, activity, or person or exhibiting other cultural or aesthetic values

Earthworks: A large-scale alteration to the landscape through excavation or piling of earth to assist with feats of engineering or in military history, used to protect against enemy fire

Emissary: A representative

Eroding: To erode, to disintegrate or slowly eat away

Indigenous: Originating in and characteristic of a particular region or country

Interpretation: An explanation or supposition of a concept, work, and/or behavior as it pertains to a specific period of time, culture, or people

Laden: To burden, weigh down, add a load

Oral traditions: Cultural and historical traditions and stories passed down by word of mouth

Post stains/Postmold stains: Small, circular stains produced when the buried ends of sapling-framed structures were removed from the ground, leaving shallow depressions that filled with organic-rich soil from a living surface. Some postmold stains formed after sapling posts rotted in place or were burned. Postmold stains can be interpreted as an architectural footprint, proving information about the size and shape of a structure (Gallivan).

Shallop: A vessel used by the colonists to navigate more shallow waters

Stockade: A defensive barrier, usually an area fortified by posts and stakes to enclose and protect occupants from outsiders

Suffused: Covered, permeated, enveloped

Tribe: A group of people united by a specified division, ties of descent, and/or community of customs and traditions

Tribute, System of Tribute: A gift, or tax, of an agreed upon resource paid to a leader or state usually in return for security, gratitude, or peace

Vassal: A subject of a superior

Weirs: A net or dam meant for catching fish

Resources

Websites and Video

America in 1607: Jamestown and the Powhatan, National Geographic http://ngm.nationalgeographic.com/static-legacy/ngm/jamestown/

The Captain John Smith Chesapeake National Historic Trail, National Park Service www.smithtrail.net

Jamestown Settlement http://www.historyisfun.org/Powhatan-Village.htm

John Smith's Adventures on the James http://206.113.151.20/johnsmithtrail/

Pocahontas Revealed, NOVA/Public Broadcasting Service http://www.pbs.org/wgbh/nova/pocahontas/

Virginia's First People: Past and Present http://virginiaindians.pwnet.org/

Virginia State Archeological Program, Virginia Department of Historic Resources http://www.dhr.virginia.gov/arch_DHR/archaeo_index.htm

Werowocomoco Research Project, College of William and Mary http://powhatan.wm.edu/

Books and Other Publications

Barbour, Philip L. *The Complete Works of Captain John Smith*. Chapel Hill: University of North Carolina Press, 1986.

Brown, Alexander. *The Genesis of the United States*. Boston: Houghton, Mifflin and Company, 1890

Egloff, Keith, and Deborah Woodward. *First People: Early Indians of Virginia*. 2nd ed. Charlottesville: University of Virginia Press, 2006.

Gallivan, Martin D., Thane Harpole, David A. Brown, Danielle Moretti-Langholtz, and E. Randolph Turner III. *The Werowocomoco (44GL32) Research Project: Background and 2003 Archeological Field Season Results.* Virginia Department of Historic Resources Research Report Series No. 17; College of William and Mary Archaeological Research Report Series No. 1, 2006.

————, E. Randolph Turner III, Justine Woodard McKnight, David A. Brown, Thane Harpole, and Danielle Moretti-Langholtz. *The Werowocomoco Research Project: 2004–2010 Field Seasons.* Virginia Department of Historic Resources Report Series; College of William and Mary Department of Anthropology Archaeological Research Report No. 3. Publication pending, 2015.

Gleach, Frederic W. *Powhatan's World and Colonial Virginia: A Conflict of Cultures.* Lincoln: University of Nebraska Press, 1997.

Haile, Edward W., ed. *Jamestown Narratives: Eyewitness Accounts of the Virginia Colony.* Champlain, VA: RoundHouse, 1998.

Moretti-Langholtz, Danielle, Ph.D., principal investigator. *A Study of Virginia Indians and Jamestown: The First Century.* Williamsburg, VA: The College of William and Mary. Prepared for the Colonial National Historical Park, National Park Service, US Department of the Interior, December 2005. Available at http://www.nps.gov/parkhistory/online_books/jame1/moretti-langholtz/index.htm

Price, David A. *Love and Hate in Jamestown: John Smith, Pocahontas, and the Heart of a New Nation.* New York: Alfred A. Knopf, 2003.

Rountree, Helen C. *Pocahontas, Powhatan, Opechancanough: Three Indian Lives Changed by Jamestown*. Charlottesville: University of Virginia Press, 2005.

———. *Pocahontas's People: The Powhatan Indians of Virginia through Four Centuries*. Norman: University of Oklahoma Press, 1990.

———. *The Powhatan Indians of Virginia: Their Traditional Culture*. Norman: University of Oklahoma Press, 1989.

———, and E. Randolph Turner III. *Before and After Jamestown: Virginia's Powhatans and Their Predecessors*. Gainesville: University of Florida Press, 2002.

———, Wayne E. Clark, and Kent Mountford. *John Smith's Chesapeake Voyages*, 1607–1609. Charlottesville: University of Virginia Press, 2007.

Townsend, Camilla. *Pocahontas and the Powhatan Dilemma*. New York: Hill and Wang, 2004.

Wood, Karenne, ed. *The Virginia Indian Heritage Trail*. 3rd ed. Charlottesville: Virginia Foundation for the Humanities, 2008. Available in print from the publisher at (434) 924-3296 or online as a digital publication at http://virginiahumanities.org/virginia-indian-program/virginia-indian-heritage-trail.

Waugaman, Sandra F., and Danielle Moretti-Langholtz, Ph.D. *We're Still Here: Contemporary Virginia Indians Tell Their Stories*. Richmond, VA: Palari Press, 2000, 2001, 2006.

Acknowledgments

The National Park Service would like to acknowledge the following individuals for their contributions to this publication.

For their passion to uncover and share the significance of Werowocomoco, Bob and Lynn Ripley;

For her visionary leadership to secure initial protection of the Werowocomoco site, and her commitment to create this handbook, former Virginia Department of Historic Resources Director Kathleen Kilpatrick;

For their talents, the creative team of author Lara Lutz; book layout and design, Virginia's Office of Graphic Communications and designer Diana Plasberg; and for the book's original illustrations, Rob Wood at Wood Ronsaville Harlin;

For their expertise, perspective, and counsel in content development and review, the Werowocomoco Research Group and the Virginia Indian Advisory Board for Werowocomoco and especially to Ken Adams, Ashley Atkins-Spivey, Wayne Adkins, David Brown, Jeff Brown, Kevin Brown, Kerry Canaday, Mark Custalow, Martin Gallivan, Thane Harpole, Lee Lockamy, Danielle Moretti-Langholtz, G. Anne Richardson, and E. Randolph Turner;

For support of the site's ongoing documentation and protection, Virginia Department of Historic Resources Director Julie V. Langan;

Contributing staff: Deanna Beacham, Suzanne Copping, Jonathan Doherty, Katherine Marks, Margaret Markham, and Abbi Wicklein-Bayne of the NPS Chesapeake Bay, and Paula Degen, Chesapeake Conservancy.

Special thanks go to Randall B. Jones, public information officer for the Virginia Department of Historic Resources for his leadership and dedication to the project, and Christine Lucero, partnership coordinator for the Captain John Smith Chesapeake National Historic Trail for her knowledge and guidance.

Index

Note: Page numbers in italics refer to captions in this name and place index.

Notes

Notes

Virginia Indians at Werowocomoco was financed, in part, with federal funds from the U.S. Department of the Interior, through the Virginia Department of Historic Resources, Commonwealth of Virginia. Under Title VI of the Civil Rights Act of 1964 and Section 504 of the Rehabilitation Act of 1973, the U.S. Department of the Interior prohibits discrimination on the basis of race, color, national origin, or disability in its federally assisted programs. If you believe that you have been discriminated against in any program or activity described herein, or if you desire further information, please write to the Office of Equal Opportunity, U.S. Department of the Interior, MS 5221 – 1949 C Street, NW, Washington, D.C. 20240. The contents and opinions of this publication do not necessarily reflect the views or policies of the Department of the Interior, nor does any mention of trade names or commercial products constitute endorsement or recommendations by the Department of the Interior. The Virginia Department of Historic Resources, in accordance with the American Disabilities Act, will make this publication available in Braille, large print, or audiotape upon request. Please allow 4 to 6 weeks for delivery.